THE LAWYER'S GUIDE TO JOB SECURITY

Also by the Author

The Lawyer's Guide to Finding Success in Any Job Market

THE LAWYER'S GUIDE TO JOB SECURITY

How to Keep Your Job—and Make the Most of It—in Good Times and Bad

RICHARD L. HERMANN

PUBLISHING

New York

Published by Kaplan Publishing, a division of Kaplan, Inc.
1 Liberty Plaza, 24th Floor
New York, NY 10006

Library of Congress Cataloging-in-Publication Data

Hermann, R. L. (Richard Lee)
   The lawyer's guide to job security : success, survival, and satisfaction in the 21st century workplace / by Richard L. Hermann.
      p. cm.
   ISBN 978-1-60714-498-4
   1. Practice of law — United States. 2. Lawyers — Job satisfaction — United States. 3. Law — Vocational guidance — United States. I. Title.
   KF300.H468 2010
   340.023'73 — dc22

                                                                    2009039770

To Anne,
who has always been indispensable to me.

Contents

Introduction

A S THIS IS BEING written, attorneys are losing their jobs at the greatest rate and in the largest numbers since such statistics began being kept. According to Lawshucks.com's Layoff Tracker, over 2,500 attorneys at top-tier law firms lost their jobs in the first six weeks of 2009. That number dramatically understates the actual number of lawyers let go during this time frame, because it does not include "stealth layoffs" (terminations that go unreported), entire law firm collapses (several major firms have recently gone under), downsizings at firms not deemed top tier, as well as corporate, government (especially state government agencies), and nonprofit layoffs. The actual number is likely several times the 2,500 cited above.

The percentage of attorneys who believe that their jobs might be in jeopardy has skyrocketed. Major law firms across the country are rescinding job offers to law students for summer associate positions at record rates. It is no surprise that lawyer anxiety is increasing.

The purpose of *The Lawyer's Guide to Job Security, Success, Survival, and Satisfaction in the 21st-Century Workplace* is to provide you with the necessary ammunition to take countermeasures against possible job loss. The book aspires to teach you how the application of some very simple, commonsense workplace principles can give you a big boost toward achieving fundamental legal career goals, which I believe are comprised of the following:

- *Security.* Insuring that when others are losing their jobs, you won't.
- *Success.* Making you result oriented so that you realize tangible achievements and accomplishments, which are the keys to promotion, higher compensation, and feelings of self-worth.
- *Survival.* Insulating you to the maximum extent against job loss, which has become of paramount importance.
- *Satisfaction.* All of the above goals contribute to getting you as close as possible to attaining what I think is the best career outcome possible, encompassed by the following axiom:

"If you find a job you like,
you will never have to work a day in your life."

One of the most important revelations to me about attorney job loss has been that an economically induced layoff is the perfect opportunity for legal employers to shed employees who are deemed dispensable. It is not the star performers who are let go unless, of course, the business collapses completely.

The 230 principles in this book were developed over almost three decades of advising attorneys on career matters and helping them surmount career crises. They are a distillation of the techniques and strategies I have counseled attorneys to employ in order to achieve the best possible legal career outcomes.

There are two common themes that run through these 200+ actionable things to make yourself indispensable, and they can be reduced to a very simple formula:

1. Common sense
2. Preparation

If you examine the underpinnings of most of these principles, you will see that they are based on these two foundations.

You do not, however, have to methodically and sequentially absorb and apply all 230 principles in this book in order to achieve indispensability (or get as close as you can to that objective). Often, as so many of my attorney clients have discovered, you reach a "take-off point" as you apply these principles to your work situation. The good habits you have instituted naturally and logically lead to additional ones that, together, contribute to indispensability.

It is my expectation that, as you absorb and incorporate these principles into your work routine, they will become second nature, your ability to "connect the dots" will increase, and indispensability will result.

Let's assume that you diligently follow every bit of advice in this book and are now deemed indispensable by your employer, who has said as much or given you other nonverbal indicators of your exalted work status. Now it is time to practice three commonsense rules, which I call the Three Rules of Indispensability.

The First Rule of Indispensability: *Never Assume That You Are Indispensable.*

Thinking of yourself as indispensable often leads to risky behavior, precisely because you have deluded yourself into thinking that, no matter what liberties you take, they would not dare let you go. Think again.

The Second Rule of Indispensability: *Always Work at Becoming Even More Indispensable.*

Once you have achieved indispensability, you will not be permitted to rest on your laurels. One of the features of the indispensable employee is that he or she keeps right on striving for excellence without letup.

The Third Rule of Indispensability: *Indispensability Breeds Very High Expectations.*

Employer expectations of indispensable employees are much higher than they are for lesser performers. Consequently, indispensability means that you must act appropriately and responsibly at all times, not only at work. Indispensable employees who do not heed this maxim tend to magnify their employer's disappointment precisely because so much is expected of them. Guess what happens then? If their behavior is particularly egregious, they soon discover that they are not quite as indispensable as they might have thought. Push the edge of the envelope of acceptable behavior at your peril.

The Corollary to the Third Rule: *A Mild Dose of Job Anxiety Is Healthy.*

It is not at all pathological for any person, no matter how much a superstar, to worry about job security. Never, ever take your job for granted. People who do tend to slack off once that they have "made it." In today's workplace, that can be a very dangerous attitude. There is simply too much uncertainty out there to ever feel totally comfortable. The bottom line usually governs every business action and applies to every single employee at every level.

Once you have arrived at the rarified level of indispensability, follow these three rules and the corollary, and you will solidify your position and be poised for even bigger triumphs.

You are never home free in the workplace. Being indispensable needs to be a way of life.

Richard L. Hermann
Arlington, Virginia
September, 2009

Chapter 1

Starting Out
on the Right Foot

*N*OTHING IS MORE IMPORTANT *than a good beginning and a great first impression. They set the stage—and the tone—for everything that follows. They lock in the positive feelings you engendered at your job interview in order to land the position in the first place. And they will boost your confidence and self-esteem.*

This chapter is designed to position you for legal job success before you walk in the door. It suggests what you need to think about before you begin the job so that you will be ready to "win" when you launch. Some of these precepts are things that you need to put in place before occupying the new position; others are things you have to organize mentally prior to going to work.

1. MAKE A GREAT FIRST IMPRESSION . . .
AND KEEP IT GOING

Psychologists and career counselors will tell you that first impressions are vitally important. In job interviews, for example, first impressions often make the difference between getting the job offer and getting the rejection slip.

According to the people who study these things, negative first impressions are also terribly difficult to overcome later. I once interviewed an applicant for a summer legal internship who had tremendous "paper" credentials: a top law school, top grades, law review, the whole nine yards. I was prepared to offer him the internship sight unseen, based on his résumé alone.

Then he walked into my office for his interview. I was shocked. He wore a shiny zip-up jacket, had obviously not combed his hair or shaved that day, had his shirttail hanging out, and after a flaccid handshake, proceeded to sit down heavily, slump down in the chair, and stare at the floor. After that stunning entrance, I did not hear a word he said. All I could think about was his slovenly appearance. And how quickly I could get him out of my office.

Ultimately, I hired a young man who ranked in the middle of his class at a very undistinguished law school. However, when he came in, he was neatly dressed, perfectly groomed, and properly respectful. *He made a great first impression.* He also turned out to be a great legal intern.

Another attorney job candidate came into my conference room and immediately took off his watch and placed it prominently on the table in front of him so that he could see the dial at all times during the interview. My first impression was of someone who had to be somewhere else and was not particularly interested in the job I had to offer. Strangely, it turned out he was very interested in the job, but after that poor first impression, I was no longer interested in him.

2. WALK TALL AND EXUDE CONFIDENCE

Image is very important, period, and even more important for lawyers in an organizational setting. A confident demeanor is critical in creating a great first impression. Confidence is also infectious. People like to be around folks—especially attorneys—who exude poise and self-assurance . . . without, of course, being overbearing.

Self-esteem, however, cannot be faked for long. And there is no reason why you should have to resort to a facade. Feeling good about yourself is a function of (1) self-discipline, (2) preparation, and (3) taking good care of yourself, both mentally and physically. If you do that, your appearance will either improve or remain at its peak level, and your mental alertness and acuity will also operate at tip-top efficiency.

Another very good reason to "look sharp, feel sharp, be sharp," to quote the old Gillette advertisement, is the stark contrast you will make with many others around you. Take stock of your colleagues and you will see that many of them mope around grousing all day long . . . and look it!

Your positive attitude and demeanor will stick out and get you noticed . . . and respected, not only by colleagues and superiors, but also by clients and prospective clients.

3. OBSERVE—AND EXCEED—THE DRESS CODE

This is a twofer.

First, observe the prevailing dress code at the office. It is always better to notice these things than to ask about them.

If you have any doubts whatsoever, assume "business conservative." You can never go wrong if, at the outset, you follow that rule. If half the men in the office wear suits and ties, and the other half come in tie-less and jacket-less, wear a suit and tie. It is more professional, you will represent your organization better at meetings with outsiders, and you will make a better impression on your supervisors, your colleagues, and your subordinates.

Second, once you have observed and noted the prevailing dress code, adhere to it every day.

Oh yes, a third bit of advice on dress: Don't ever dress down when everyone else is dressing up. Furthermore, body piercings are out, unless you work at the MTV general counsel's office.

When in doubt, go conservative, even if your organization's politics are somewhere to the left of Ralph Nader. You can never go wrong if you adhere to this principle.

4. GET—AND STAY—IN SHAPE

Contrary to popular myth, people *can* and invariably *do* judge a book by its cover. Your physical appearance means a lot. Forget the philosophical angst over whether physical appearance should or should not matter. That's a waste of time. The reality is that it does.

Whatever your current physical condition, you can do a lot to become more physically fit and vigorous. And that is always a big boost in the job market as well as with respect to business development. If it was not, we would not be reading about how employers allegedly discriminate against obese applicants.

Physical fitness is worth the effort on a lot of levels, not the least of which has to do with your job. In addition to making you look better and boosting your self-esteem, it will provide you with more energy and enthusiasm. It also will make a strong and favorable impression on your coworkers, bosses, professional colleagues, prospective employers, customers, internal and external clients, and everyone else with whom you will come into contact.

Individuals with disabilities, even those with visible disabilities, can also profit from fitness programs. I know a very successful paraplegic attorney at the U.S. Department of Justice who swims a mile three days a week *before* he drives across town to play wheelchair basketball! He looks and acts terrific and is brimming with self-confidence and charisma. After a while, you forget that he is in a wheelchair.

5. ALWAYS BE WELL GROOMED

This should go without saying, but so should a lot of the other commonsense precepts about attorney behavior. Unfortunately, they ALL have to be said. Such is the nature of human nature and of the 21st-century workplace.

One of my attorneys came to work unshaven at least one day a week. In addition to looking like he had been on an overnight bender (I found out much later that he had been!), his shabby appearance said a lot to me about both his self-esteem and his respect for me and my organization. He did not last long.

This kind of *faux pas* may seem like a little one to you, but the little ones add up. And they usually go together. Mr. Unkempt, for example, usually neglected to wear a tie (notwithstanding that every other male legal career counselor in the office always wore one) and went around with his top one or two shirt buttons undone. In short, he looked like a slob.

Looks, by the way, are not always deceiving. In his case, sloppy personal habits were reflected in sloppy work habits. Mr. Unkempt was not the greatest performer on the job. In fact, he was one of the worst. But not for long.

At about the same time, I had a female attorney employee who always came to work looking exceptionally well groomed. It was obvious that she took time every morning to make sure she looked presentable. She was also a marginal performer, but my attitude toward her work performance was 180 degrees opposite to how I felt about Mr. Unkempt. I was perfectly willing to be patient with her until she was able to upgrade her on-the-job performance, mainly because she made a great impression on everyone.

Good grooming these days means more than what it used to mean. In addition to the more conventional governing principles, this must also be said: cover up your tattoos.

6. BE POSITIVE AND UPBEAT

Aside from the obvious, there is one overpowering reason to walk around being upbeat. Influential management consultants who have the ear of law firm managing partners and C-level corporate executives are advising their clients as follows: if you have to cut people, cut the ones with low morale and the glum ones who adversely affect the rest of the staff, not to mention clients.

Everyone likes an optimist, regardless of his or her other shortcomings. President Ronald Reagan may not have been the most intelligent, knowledgeable, or hardworking chief executive, but he was successful and very popular nevertheless, largely because he always exuded tremendous optimism.

No one enjoys being around a bitter person or someone who whines and complains all the time.

Besides, it feels a whole lot better to be positive than negative.

7. BE FRIENDLY

Nothing is worse, more discouraging, and less enjoyable than being around a grouch. It is no fun to have to walk around an office on eggshells for fear of arousing the ire of the office malcontent.

If you are subject to serious mood swings or Churchillian "black dog" days, maybe working around other people is not for you. It is certainly not for anyone else who has to work alongside you in the same environment. If this describes you, perhaps solo practice or telecommuting is more to your taste.

I once hired an attorney who, from day one, manifested major grouchlike tendencies. Being new in business, I made the mistake of tolerating her negativism for too long, making futile attempts to get her to relax, lighten up, and fit in. Eventually, I had to let her go because she made everyone else so uncomfortable. Her very presence impeded office productivity. Once she left, morale improved severalfold and the office became a much happier—and considerably more productive—workplace.

Two additional reasons to be friendly:

1. It takes less effort than being mad all the time.
2. It is far less stressful.

8. DON'T ACT WEIRD

A new employee of a multinational corporation's in-house counsel office began his first day of work like this: He arrived in a convoy, driving his own car and followed by two rental trucks containing over 100 boxes of his "important files." After he parked his car, he sauntered into his boss's office and asked where the movers he had hired could unload the boxes.

Instantly, the new guy was labeled as weird. The boss began to have serious second thoughts about his hiring decision. It was going to take a very long time for the new employee to overcome this wacky first impression. He never did.

Your first day is perhaps the most important day you will spend on a job. Day one is when you are being initially assessed and judged by your coworkers and your supervisors and subordinates. First impressions are often lasting impressions. They are tough, if not impossible, to overcome.

If you act normal and "mainstream," you will have no difficulty getting through this initial scrutiny. Act otherwise and you will quickly become a talked-about legend . . . for all the wrong reasons.

9. TAKE IT SLOW

It is often tempting to come into a job, immediately see things that you believe could be improved, and feel the urge to go to the boss and dazzle him or her with your insightful and innovative recommendations.

Resist the temptation, at least for the moment. Until you have been with the organization for a while, you will not have earned sufficient credibility to be in a position to make suggestions. Bide your time. If you make a good first impression and keep it going by solid performance, the time will soon come when you can confidently advocate for your suggested improvements and actually be listened to with interest.

Until then, keep a low profile when it comes to promoting improvements. Who knows, you may learn something about the business that causes you to feel relieved that you did not leap into the fray right away.

10. GROUND YOURSELF IN REALITY

Benvenuto Cellini was one of those rare "Renaissance men" of 16th-century Italy, an accomplished sculptor, author, playwright, soldier, poet, etc., and a man who thought very highly of himself. Early one morning, he was walking with a friend while the dew was still clinging to the grass. It was a sunny day, and as Cellini looked down at the ground in front of him, he saw to his amazement that his shadow sported a halo around his head, while that of his companion did not. This nimbus convinced him beyond any lingering doubt that he was, truly, very special, someone around whom the world and the sun and the planets revolved.

A nice illusion. One that most of us, deep down, share. The only problem is, it isn't true. What Cellini saw was an optical illusion that you can confirm very easily yourself. The Germans, who label things better than anyone else, call this false halo *Heiligenschein,* the "holy aura."

Cellini was a very bright fellow, but not that special. If you share his illusion, get over it. You will be better served in the long run by an understanding of, and appreciation for, where you really stand in the world.

In order to survive and advance in a cold, impersonal, and often brutal working world, you have to be a realist. A realist is someone who sees the world as it is, not as he or she wants it to be.

This does not mean that you should not have realistic aspirations regarding what you can accomplish. You only have to realize that these aspirations will not be achieved automatically. It is going to take some effort on your part.

11. TAKE NOTHING FOR GRANTED

Whenever you join a new organization, you are bound to hear a lot of tales about organizational culture, policies, procedures, etc. Always consider the source of the information before you accept it as gospel.

Five minutes after I arrived at my permanent Army duty station in Germany one lazy summer Sunday afternoon, a very large, loud, authoritative man walked in my room wearing "full-bird" colonel's eagles on his shoulders. I leaped to attention, whereupon he proceeded to inspect me, my uniform, and my duffel bag, which I had just thrown on top of my cot. He made a big show of the inspection, after which he lectured me about the rules of unit behavior, all of which sounded both intimidating and impossible to remember or comply with. Then he did a crisp about-face and left. I sat there stunned, my hopes for an easy transition into the unit dashed.

I attempted to get my personal possessions in order in accordance with the colonel's instructions. The next morning at my first formation, I discovered that the "colonel" was, in fact, a private first class who I outranked and who was putting one over on the newbie. I should have noticed that the faux colonel was much too young by at least 20 years to be sporting eagles on his shoulders. But I did not, fixated instead on the eagles themselves and the authoritative demeanor of the imposter.

This does not mean that you have to be skeptical about absolutely everything. You don't. But if something does not strike you as authentic, it probably is not. The eyes rarely lie.

12. BE HONEST

I know an attorney who has made a cottage industry out of telling lies and embellishments in order to create and maintain a Potemkin village–type facade of success and influence. Grigori Potemkin was Russian Czarina Catherine the Great's prime minister who created illusions of peasant prosperity all along the Volga one season when Catherine decided to tour her empire by barge. Each village along the riverbank was camouflaged by false fronts made up to look as terrific and authentic as Hollywood movie sets, hiding the squalor behind them.

When this attorney meets someone for the *second* time, he has a hard time remembering which lie or exaggeration he told that particular person the *first* time they met.

Also, in the early days of the mobile telephone, he would go to meetings with a big, bulky phone on his shoulder and instruct his office to call him every 30 minutes so that he would look important. In fact, he looked ridiculous.

Trust in an employee can disappear in the face of dishonesty. I once asked one of my law clerks to go to a print shop, pick up a big job, and insert the freshly copied pages into notebooks for an important presentation we were about to make, and *to make sure they were inserted in the correct sequence.* Much to my embarrassment,

I found out later that a large number of them had been inserted out of order. When confronted with his obvious error, the law clerk insisted that he had checked every single page. Following that, he went on my watch list, and my trust in him collapsed completely. Fortunately, he was only a summer clerk, so he was soon gone.

Sooner or later, dissembling is bound to end in humiliation or worse for the perpetrator. So don't do it.

Another, more important reason to stick to the truth is that reputation is basically all an attorney has left after everything else has been stripped away. A reputation for integrity is the best professional legal reputation of all and one that will ultimately reward you. In a world where we have come to expect that all of our institutional leaders often lie to us, a reputation for integrity will stand out.

I recently advised the chief lawyer for a Fortune 500 corporation on his career. I was very impressed with him as an individual during our meeting. When I expressed that impression to members of my staff after the attorney left the office, one employee remarked that he had observed this paragon of the legal profession stealing one of our publications when he thought no one was watching him. Needless to say, my opinion of him was radically revised.

13. THINK CAREER . . . NOT JUST JOB

How often have you heard an unemployed family member or friend say: "I just want a *job!*"? Conversely, how often have you heard someone say: "I just want a *career!*"? Probably never.

A career is much better than a job. Careers contain within them many jobs and job options, sometimes millions of them. If you think in terms of *career,* then plan your attack on the job market with your *career* in mind, you probably will never be unemployed for long. You will probably also be a much happier camper in any job.

Thinking career rather than job also forces you to plan ahead and to keep up with developments in your career field. This will also provide you the early warning system everyone needs today in order to avoid hurtling over the job security abyss.

14. KNOW WHAT YOU WANT TO DO "THE DAY AFTER"

Ten years ago, I advised those rare legal career counseling candidates that evidenced too much job-hopping on their résumés to try to camouflage that instability, if possible. I also tended to summarily reject any job applicant if he or she demonstrated job-hopping tendencies.

Now the scenario has changed. Job-hopping, as I was accustomed to defining it, is commonplace, rendered so by an economy gone inside out and transforming itself rapidly. When I ask applicants why they held four jobs in two years, the answers are often quite legitimate:

> *"Law firm A went out of business . . . company B was acquired by Aggressive Sharks, Inc., and my legal office was eliminated as redundant . . . company C went through a downsizing after losing its defense contract . . . and company D filed under Chapter 11 of the Bankruptcy Code and is attempting to reorganize."*

Consequently, I am much less doctrinaire today about hiding the sad fact of job-hopping.

Bouncing around in a volatile economy is rapidly becoming a fact of life for an awful lot of attorneys and others. Unfortunately, despite their own personal experiences with sudden and frequent job changes, the overwhelming majority of job-hopping candidates who come to me for legal career transition counseling still have not gotten the idea that they have to plan for the worst case.

Always have a plan in mind, in case the worst case happens. These days, it often does.

15. EXPECT THE UNEXPECTED

The unexpected is part of both personal and professional life. Very little turns out as we anticipate.

So how come most of us are utterly unprepared to cope with unanticipated consequences when they hit us in the face? Without delving into chaos theory, the unexpected is eminently predictable, so get used to it. Even the attacks of September 11, 2001, were not totally unexpected by smart, forward-thinking people who took time to examine and write about trends in worldwide terrorism. There were even a few FBI agents who managed to connect the dots. Tragically, no one in a responsible position paid any attention to them. Rather, they foolishly took it for granted that Fortress America, insulated by two vast oceans from most of the ills afflicting the rest of the planet, would be forever safe and secure.

On a more mundane level, most people begin a new task, a new job, even a new marriage or the arrival of a new baby on something of a high. "Hey, this is going to be great!" Reality soon sets in: the task is more complicated than it appeared to be; the new job and the new coworkers aren't so terrific; the new spouse is sloppy, disinterested, etc.; the baby cries all night and wakes up at inopportune times. These realities often hit like a ton of bricks, and we crumple beneath the barrage.

However, if you know from the beginning that you have to factor in a certain amount of the unforeseen, mindful that the unexpected is normal, the more you will be able to cope with it successfully and move on.

Challenges are usually predictable, so predict them. Make contingency plans designed to get you through the rough spots. Getting anything worthwhile done right is difficult enough if everything goes according to plan. Assume that you will be surprised somewhere along the line.

This more realistic view flies in the face of all the feel-good literature and motivational products clamoring for your attention.

Worrying in advance about unforeseen developments—factoring them into your thought processes and planning—is an eminently intelligent (read: realistic) perspective that will serve you well all your life. While others collapse at the first sign of adversity, you will be ready to put your positivistic action plan into high gear, roll with the punches, and get over the hump.

16. MAKE LISTS

I have three lists that I have maintained for over 30 years:

- *A work calendar,* in which I list the things I must do each day. Ideally, I do this the night before, and then prioritize activities when I first arrive at work the next morning.

- *A personal calendar,* in which I record the following information:
  - The things I have to accomplish each day in my personal life.
  - Any ideas, interesting thoughts, intriguing quotes, books I would like to read, movies I want to see, and my exercise results for the day (largely swimming).

    I keep my personal calendar on my bed stand at night, having discovered that some of my best—or at least most intriguing—ideas come to me when I am either about to drift off to sleep or wake up.

- *An idea notebook,* in which I transcribe the ideas I have logged in my daily calendar. I do this at the end of each month and elaborate on the ideas in more detail. Over the years, many of these ideas have provided the basis for the things I have undertaken and successfully accomplished at work and elsewhere. In fact, my entire business derived from an idea I put in my notebook over 30 years ago.

I'm not mandating that you have to adopt the same approach. I only provide my technique of keeping track of things because it is the way that works for me. You may find that a variation on this theme works better for you. Great!

The point is that we live in a complex, fast-moving, frenzied world, and keeping some semblance of order vis-à-vis your environment is very important. This is just one way to achieve a modicum of order.

17. LEARN AS MUCH AS YOU CAN ABOUT THE ORGANIZATION

This is something you can—and should—start doing even *before* you begin work. Whether you examine materials about your new employer on the Internet, request them from the employer's public affairs office, or consult a reference librarian at the public library, the opportunity is there to become a reasonably well-informed new hire by the time you report for your first day of work. The more you know, the easier the transition into the new workplace and the more rapidly you will be able to hit the ground running. This will impress your bosses with your competence while contributing to that great first impression.

Chapter 2

Building Your Value to the Organization

*C*ONGRATULATIONS! YOU GOT *the job. You dutifully followed the advice in chapter 1 about preparing yourself to shine when you begin work. Now you can relax.*

Not just yet.

Now is the time to get your ducks in a row and make sure you are prepared to take the steps necessary to make that terrific first impression on your new bosses and colleagues and demonstrate that your employer did not make a mistake when he or she hired you. Applying this advice will also establish a platform for both job security and advancement in the organization.

Winning the job is no guarantee you will succeed in doing it. Often, the job description that you read in the newspaper or had described to you in the interview omitted some very important information. Or the job priorities were not pointed out with quite the clarity you discover during your first day at work. This is where you make up ground for what you might have missed in the run-up to the position.

Chapter 2 includes advice geared both to immediate job success and to beginning to build credibility with your superiors, colleagues, and support staff. It also advises about justification for retaining you if and when the legal office hits hard times.

18. STUDY THE EMPLOYEE HANDBOOK

Many employers have formal employee handbooks. Large employers generally go at least one step further and have employee handbooks that are both detailed and exhaustive and that have been crafted by legal counsel in conjunction with human resources.

Employee handbooks are well worth early attention from you. The more you absorb and understand what is in them, the better you will be able to manage your legal career to your advantage.

During my first month at the Pentagon, I went to the Pentagon Law Library and spent several hours reading the *Federal Personnel Manual* and its Department of Defense and Office of the Secretary of Defense (OSD) supplemental rules and regulations. Several years later, when OSD downsized and many of its 700+ employees were at risk of losing their jobs, that base knowledge of personnel rules—and the fact that my supervisors knew that I was one of the few individuals on board who had read them—came in very handy. I was even asked to become the informal advisor to the OSD Personnel Office on the employment law aspects of the downsizing.

Typical employee handbooks are very informative, covering such key topics as organizational values, mission, goals, policies, and procedures; pay and benefits; performance expectations; professional behavioral expectations; EEO and harassment policies; employee grievance procedures; ethics and codes of conduct; employee discipline; confidentiality and email and employee privacy; noncompete covenants; implementation of the Family and

Medical Leave Act and the Americans with Disabilities Act; disability accommodation; recruiting preferences for internal candidates; access to personnel records; dress codes; severance policies, etc.

19. LEARN ALL OF THE RULES

I once worked for an organization that was forced to go through a downsizing. It was called a reduction in force (RIF) and was governed by an elaborate set of rules and regulations that were boring and intimidating to read, but devastating to those employees who had never bothered to make the effort to find out what they said.

Without exception, it was the employees who knew the personnel and related rules and understood their rights who survived the RIF and, in certain cases, even benefited from it. The ones who were too lazy to have ever bothered with these dry documents paid for their laxity by becoming the victims of the downsizing.

As with most personnel and other regulations in large organizations, there was enough uncertainty, ambiguity, and plain illogic and poor drafting that a knowledgeable person could save his or her job if he or she had read and contemplated the rules and loopholes.

One of the most important things a new employee can do is to learn, in detail, the rules and regulations that govern the organization. Employees who don't do this are far more likely to become workplace casualties than their more farsighted and ambitious colleagues who take the time (their *own* time, not company time, of course) to know how the place functions.

20. LEARN THE BUZZWORDS

Every organization and industry has its special language. When I first went to work at the Pentagon, I was overwhelmed by the volume of new words and hundreds of acronyms that I had never encountered before. Fortunately, I came across a book entitled *The Dictionary of U.S. Government Acronyms* and grabbed a copy as quickly as I could. It was a lifesaver, as well as an easy means of acquiring insider knowledge and status. Soon I was able to differentiate between ROPMA and DOPMA and throw around DMDC and CHAMPUS with seasoned veterans of the aptly named Puzzle Palace.

Learn your organization's unique language quickly so that you will be able to converse knowledgeably about important issues. Just remember to keep this inside jargon out of your résumé should you seek employment outside the organization or industry in the future. Nothing is more annoying to a prospective employer than a résumé or candidate presentation that resorts to the esoteric lingua franca of the applicant's workplace.

Why do organizations develop unique modes of expression? Some of it is unavoidable. After all, language differentiations evolved in the first place because populations organized themselves by proximity or by division of labor. Some of it is due to isolation from the rest of the world. Most, however, develops because it creates an aura of mystery, of "us versus them," and creates a group of insiders—a "priesthood"—with membership rituals and exclusionary rules that immediately distinguish and elevate the guild members from the community of "nonbelievers." Every organization is guilty of this, which may be one reason we all have so much difficulty communicating clearly with one another.

Some of us become so immersed in the inside idiom of our workplace that we tend to forget completely how the rest of the world speaks. I was reminded of this when a friend of mine who ran a Russian exchange program invited me to a dinner for his Russian counterpart. A State Department translator was present to help us understand each other. After several hours and many Vodka toasts, we managed to communicate very well without any intermediation. Leaving the dinner, I was struck by the contrast between this event and similar ones where I was put together with people who, presumably, grew up in the United States, but spoke a foreign language—the language of their workplace. They had forgotten how to communicate with other people in plain English. If any event needed a professional translator, it was this variety.

You also need to be up on certain other buzzwords that achieve temporary notoriety, if only to be in the know. Take "multitasking," for example. Multitasking is just another way of saying keeping more than one ball in the air simultaneously, or being able to chew gum and walk at the same time. It is not a big deal, but it has achieved an exalted status as I write this chapter. You see it everywhere—job descriptions, classified job ads, internal memos. Like most terminology fads, it is soon likely to join "total quality management" and "zero-based budgeting" in the dustbin of linguistic history.

Hyphenated terms that don't really mean very much are tremendously popular among human resources staff and managers everywhere: "team-building," "fast-paced," and "world-class," to name a few. You get the idea. While real folks tend to laugh at this mode of expression, the managerial class takes it very seriously. That means that you should at least know what the powers-that-be think they mean, even if you think they're meaningless.

21. KNOW THE PRODUCTS AND SERVICES

This should be obvious, but if it were, then I would not always have been so frustrated when new employees joined my company and, after several months, still asked the most basic, first-day questions about what we did.

You can learn about your organization's products and services by performing an Internet search and also by reading product literature produced by both the organization and outside firms.

22. IDENTIFY THE SOUL OF THE ORGANIZATION

Along with all the other very important early tasks you should tackle in order to scope out your organization and secure your niche in it, you should take some time to dissect the outfit in order to get to its core essence. Every organization has an essence, a soul if you will (although many of my clients who came out of major law firms might dispute that), something that is of paramount importance to it. It is surprising how many times employees, even long-time employees, are utterly clueless as to what this essence might be.

During my Pentagon stint, I met a great many senior naval (among other military) officers and civilian employees. I was constantly befuddled by their behavior, until it struck me one day that I had completely misconstrued the essence of the navy, which I had incorrectly assumed to be projecting massive sea power throughout the world in order to intimidate and scare off the Soviet Navy. Wrong!

The real essence of the navy, I discovered, was to achieve supremacy over its archrival services, the air force and the army, particularly the former. The best brains in the navy worried about ways to keep the navy ahead of the air force when it came to competing for budget money and weapons systems. The second-best navy brains worried about mundane things like sea power projection, two-and-a-half ocean wars, and the Soviet threat.

23. MASTER THE ORGANIZATIONAL STRUCTURE

Find an organization chart and study it thoroughly. If one does not exist, develop one for yourself. If there are mission statements available, study them, too. Know which office reports to which other office and which one is more important than the others.

In larger organizations, this may require a more elaborate effort than merely studying and memorizing an organization chart. You actually have to walk around and examine the physical setting in which these offices do their work. Some offices, you will find, are more equal than others, even if the people in them are of comparable rank or even of lesser rank.

In large organizations in particular, not every job title or position in the hierarchy equates to real power. Keeping your eyes and ears open will quickly identify the true power centers. This will enable you to know where to go for advice and assistance and who to watch in order to avoid being stabbed in the back.

There was, for example, a Pentagon civilian of fairly modest rank who had an enormous office, of a size customarily reserved for an assistant secretary of defense. How he, several levels below an assistant secretary, got an office like that, I did not know. But that was irrelevant. He had it, and in as rank-obsessed an environment as the Pentagon, that was all that mattered. The man had clout disproportionate to his rank, and I knew early on that I would have to respect that.

It turned out that this individual had been there a long time and had very shrewdly nurtured the urban legend that he had amassed an extensive file of information—some of it not so flattering—about many of the people who outranked him as well as on certain members of Congress. His job put him in a great position to gather juicy information on inside-the-beltway people, should he have been so inclined. By the time I arrived at the Pentagon, it did not matter whether the rumors about his secret files were true or not. No one wanted to risk confirming them. In short, he was a mini J. Edgar Hoover.

While this Pentagon office size discrepancy was clearly a special case, there are more ordinary circumstances where physical inspection of the organization yields useful information. Take a look at a White House organization chart. It is full of special assistants, deputy assistants, principal deputy assistants, confidential assistants, and so forth. It is impossible to determine where they rank relative to one another. Their job titles sound like clones of each other. But note where their offices are in relation to the Oval Office and you will have surmised a great deal about who the important people are and who the less significant players are.

The same thing holds true in every organization. The closer the office to the seat of ultimate power, the more important the occupant.

An attorney friend of mine once went to work for a large corporation and naturally assumed that his immediate boss, the corporate general counsel, was the individual he had to worry about and please. Imagine his shock when he was verbally assaulted in a meeting by the chief financial officer while his lawyer boss slunk into a corner and tried to make herself invisible.

Frequently, all is not as it appears to be on the organization chart. If the CFO has the general counsel in his pocket and is really pulling the legal department strings, that is unusual. Nevertheless, this is important information that should have been learned early enough to avoid trouble.

How do things like this happen? In some outfits, the organization chart gets suspended because someone is the relative of one of the organizational honchos. In other places, it could be based on who is bedding down with whom. In some places, it is simply a matter of the clash of wills and the prevailing of one will or personality over another. Regardless, it behooves you to find this stuff out and behave accordingly.

24. DETERMINE WHO WIELDS THE
REAL POWER

Louis XIV, the Sun King of France, was the supreme monarch of his era. But the real power behind the throne was his Eminence

Grise, Louis's Gray Eminence, Cardinal Richelieu. It was the cardinal who was the real power and the germinator of virtually every governmental policy and pronouncement that issued from Louis's hand.

In the British system, the number two person in each government ministry, the permanent secretary (official title: Permanent Under-Secretary of State) is a career official—the ministry's most senior civil servant—who serves as the gray eminence for the political cabinet minister. The minister is a transient figure, typically in the job for only a few years. The permanent secretary is there for the duration. It is this individual who knows how the department really operates and where the bodies are buried. The minister is virtually forced to rely on him or her for almost everything he or she attempts.

The same holds true in many U.S. organizations. Time in the job equals a depth of knowledge that the C-level (CEO, COO, CFO, CIO, CLO, etc.) people simply cannot equal. Hence, they are forced to rely heavily on underlings. In the 32 years since the U.S. Department of Energy has been in existence, for example, it has had 12 secretaries of energy and numerous general counsels, but only one deputy general counsel, a man acknowledged by everyone to wield enormous power over every legal activity and input into the business of the department. He is both the institutional history and institutional memory of the entire department.

25. STUDY THE ORGANIZATIONAL HISTORY

It has become popular among companies and other organizations in recent years to document their histories. These are numbingly dull reads, but immensely valuable sources of information for new employees. If you read them, you will likely know more about the organization than virtually anyone else. Especially since you will probably be the only person who ever bothered to read the document.

If you work in the public sector, you have a tremendous opportunity to become an expert on your organization. Most government agencies are established by legislation (a few derive from executive orders of the president), and most legislation is accompanied by extensive legislative histories, all of which are either available on department and agency websites or in their libraries (try the *U.S. Congressional Code and Administrative News,* an excellent source of legislative histories).

An online literature search should uncover material written by outsiders who are likely to have a very different point of view than the organization man or woman who wrote the in-house publication.

It is also important to realize that most organizations that have been around for a while have at least a few skeletons in their closets. Your historical study may uncover some of them. Others may emerge through your literature search. It is always useful to have this intelligence. Perhaps the finest example of this kind of intelligence gathering was long-time FBI director J. Edgar Hoover, who had enough on everyone above him to achieve the ultimate in job security. While I am not suggesting that you model yourself on Mr. Hoover, it never hurts to know what is going on in your organization.

26. KNOW WHAT IS IMPORTANT TO MANAGEMENT

Bosses evaluate every event and activity in terms of their business impact. They may be the most compassionate people on earth, but they cannot help filtering everything they encounter through its bottom-line impact.

If you know this fact when you start work, you will be light years ahead of your colleagues, many of whom will never figure it out. Consequently, you will be able to gauge your movements and talking points against their impact on the bosses' thought processes—what is considered most important by management.

Survival is what is most important to management in every organization. Survival of both the manager(s) and the organization, since without the latter, there will be no former. After that, items deemed important vary considerably. Advancement is almost always paramount for every manager, although there are exceptions—usually those individuals who have either arrived in a comfort zone that they do not wish to relinquish or those rare persons who realize that they have achieved their Peter Principle ceiling level of competence.

In a publicly traded company, the quarterly financials are extremely important. Less so in a closely held company. Law firms often focus laserlike on partner profits versus their competitors; government agencies focus on making their political appointees, and ultimately, the chief executive, look good and get reelected.

27. KNOW HOW THE BOSSES THINK

Aligning your workplace thinking with your bosses' up the chain of command can pay big benefits. People naturally tend to conclude that those who think like they do are a special breed, exalted above all others.

Finding out how the bosses think is not as difficult as it might seem. Organizations nowadays flood their employees and customers with information in the form of websites, releases, blogs, publications, and other messages. Many of these are archived, providing you with a gold mine of information about the thought processes of your superiors.

In addition, there are so many media outlets competing for attention that it is likely that if you Google your bosses' names, you will return interviews with them, as well as other communications that allow you to peer into their skulls for insights into who they really are.

28. UNDERSTAND ENOUGH TO EXPLOIT
THE TECHNOLOGY

I started my company in the pre–desktop computer era, a time when I learned and knew literally every aspect of the business. A short time later, we obtained our first desktop computers and immediately discovered that we needed both internal and external assistance to properly maintain the equipment.

The advent of the Internet, Web technology, email, et al. was another blow to my original intent to know everything that went on in the business. During its last 10 years, I became so reliant on our technical staff and outside technology consultants that I often felt like a mere cipher while they actually controlled what went on in the company.

This is not a position in which you want to find yourself. However, looking at it from the other side, understanding enough of the technology that runs your organization so that (1) you can maximize its utility for yourself and (2) you can become a first-line resource for your work colleagues is not a bad place to be if you want to make yourself indispensable.

A perfect example is the attorney who was let go by his law firm and referred by the firm to me for outplacement. He happened to mention during our initial intake consultation that he was something of a computer geek and informally advised members of the firm who would come to him with computer problems. However, upon further probing, it became evident that the firm managers knew nothing about his computer skills. I suggested that we recraft his résumé to give them prominence and that he propose to the firm that he move into a technology position, pointing out that his legal knowledge combined with his computer skills made him a valuable resource. I also had him collect testimonials from firm partners, associates, and support staff whom he had helped with technology issues and append them to the résumé. Once the firm managers were made aware of his computer talents, they created a new position of "legal technology manager" and moved him into it.

This does not mean that you have to take home those turgid and incomprehensible computer manuals in either print or electronic format. All you have to do is know how to use the software that serves you so that you become adept with it. Ideally, you should be able to troubleshoot if something impedes its use, and let your colleagues know that you can help them with technology problems.

29. BE PROFESSIONAL

This is one of the most important rules in this book. Like Supreme Court Justice Potter Stewart's famous comment about obscenity—"I can't define it, but I know it when I see it"—being professional is not easy to define. If you implement the recommendations in this book, you will have no problem achieving and maintaining a high standard of professionalism.

Unprofessional behavior, in contrast, is almost always very easy to spot, and that is what you have to watch out for. Despite its ambiguous nature, being professional is fundamental to success in the working world.

Amateurs lose out to professionals in every endeavor, with few exceptions, whether it's looking for a new job, advancing in their current position, playing a sport, or anything else. To be truly professional, you have to keep ahead of the knowledge curve. You must constantly educate yourself about your organization, your industry, your competitors, and everything else for which you have time.

This means you will have to do some work at home on your own time. This is not the kind of thing you should be doing on company time.

There is also a behavioral aspect to professionalism: civility, courtesy, presentation, and keeping your cool.

30. BE ON TIME . . . AND STAY A LITTLE LATE

Come in a little early your first day on the new job. Subsequently, make sure you arrive at work punctually, at the latest. A 9:00 A.M. to 5:00 P.M. workday does not begin at 9:15. It begins at 9:00.

Also, don't leave work at the instant the clock strikes 5:00. And don't begin preparing to depart until the actual end of the workday.

Both early arrival and late departure can have a very positive effect on your career because of what they say to your bosses, one or more of whom are likely to come in early and leave late themselves. The primary reason for this is that the work ethic has deteriorated in most organizations, and very few people arrive on time or stay one minute after hours. You will stick out.

Attorneys, particularly in major law firms, tend to work long hours anyway. In fact, young associates often go to an extreme, fearful of leaving before the senior attorneys and partners depart for the evening (or should I say, night?). If you do your work well and in a timely fashion, you do not have to do this. Although billable hours are important, if you achieve the annual threshold number of billable hours, you do not have to strain yourself to go beyond that number. You will ultimately be judged on the quality of your work to a much greater extent than the amount of time you sit at your desk.

Moreover, the reign of the billable hour might be short-lived, given both increased client sophistication and awareness of legal billing practices and the severe economic stress under which virtually every business now operates.

31. GIVE (AT LEAST) A DAY'S WORK FOR A DAY'S PAY

The number of people who don't follow this simple precept is astonishing, and employers are not happy about it. During my first week in my first job after law school, I was taken aside by a colleague and told that, by staying late, I was setting a bad example; others might also be expected to stay beyond the 5:00 p.m. close of business. I was undeterred. After all, my colleague was not going to be the arbiter of my performance.

When it comes to contemplating hard work, just do it and you will ultimately be rewarded handsomely.

32. KEEP YOUR TURF—AND YOURSELF— NEAT, CLEAN, ORGANIZED, AND LOOKING GOOD

This means your office, desk area, files, bookshelves, etc. If you come across like a slob, everyone will assume you are one.

I once hired an attorney directly out of a prestigious federal government honors employment program, her first job out of law school. She came to the interview dressed in a conservative business suit well tailored for her figure. Her first day on the job, she walked into her office, threw her overcoat on the floor, and took off her shoes. My opinion of her immediately took a nosedive . . . and stayed down there.

Her performance on the job was consistent with her slovenly behavior. Consequently, she did not last very long.

Keeping your personal work space neat, clean, and orderly sets a positive tone, not only for you, but for everyone else with whom you come into contact. You will find that your coworkers tend to avoid coming to see you if your office looks like it was hit by a Category Five hurricane.

Organizing your work intelligently and neatly is not as easy as it sounds. Papers tend to pile up in inboxes, and every passing day accumulates more of it. The same is true of emails. Try to dispose of them each day before you leave work.

Don't dress like a slob, either. Be professional. If your organization institutes a casual dress day, that is not a license to come in looking like you play lead guitar for a heavy metal band.

Image may not be everything, but it sure counts for a lot.

33. KEEP YOUR COOL AT ALL TIMES

This is a critical rule for getting along and getting ahead in the workplace. It is also one of the toughest to follow. Humans are naturally emotional beings. Unfortunately, any emotional outburst at work can harm your career, since it will be perceived by others as not being professional. Hence, it is best to remember at all times to rein in your emotions. Keep them under control, no matter what the provocation. You must remind yourself to look and act professional even in the most emotionally charged circumstances.

Two of the attorneys who worked for me did not like each other and, as time passed, made their mutual hostility evident. Despite my counseling them about their problem, the antipathy escalated until, one day, it resulted in a fist fight. It did not matter to me "who started it." I could not countenance an office so disrupted by the petty grievances of one employee toward another. Both were gone within weeks.

People who don't keep their emotions in check and behave with proper decorum quickly lose the respect of their coworkers. Going bonkers is a sign of weakness and uncertainty, if not panic. Don't ever let your colleagues see you that way.

Emulating President Obama in this respect might be a good idea. He has honed the "rule of cool" as well as anyone.

34. ASSUME NOTHING

Don't follow the lead of economists, who are trained early on to assume things where they don't exist. If an economist were stranded on a desert island and wanted to start a fire to cook raw meat, the joke goes, he would assume a match. Maybe this mode of thinking is why corporations are filling up the streets of America with fired economists.

It is very dangerous to your career to proceed on the basis of anything other than verifiable fact. Assuming something is reckless and shows that you are hopelessly naive, not an impression you ever want to leave with anyone.

I gave a speech several years ago and arrived at the assembly hall approximately five minutes before I was supposed to go on. I was just in time to hear no less an authority than the general counsel (i.e., the chief attorney) of a large U.S. government cabinet department pronounce to the audience: "I assure you that, in two weeks, the Standard Form 171, the government's universal employment application form, will be history." That turned out to be complete hogwash, as anyone tuned into reality and not operating on the basis of assumption could have told the audience (I did). She assumed that outcome on the basis of a rumor that came to her ear from a purportedly credible source. Unfortunately, she never took the time to check out the rumor for herself, which proved a precursor for the way she would continue to conduct herself during her brief tenure in government. This general counsel lost her job after embarrassing herself before a congressional committee when she admitted to making many more serious—and equally erroneous—assumptions that got her into deep trouble.

This kind of stuff goes on all the time throughout the world of work. And it invariably gets the "assumers" into trouble. Too bad, when all they had to do was exercise some restraint until they ferreted out the truth.

35. MAINTAIN A SUPPLY OF BUSINESS CARDS

If your employer does not supply them, invest in your own. The major office supply retailers enable you to design your own business cards online, offering a wide variety of templates that you can personalize. Most of them permit you to design and pick up your business cards the same day, from a retail location close to where you live or work. Alternatively, you can have them shipped to you.

Always carry your business cards with you ... and hand them out lavishly, at every opportunity.

This is important not only for your immediate professional development, but also for your future, should it become necessary to consider leaving the organization. Continuous legal career management is vitally important in today's uncertain workplace and economy. Every time you meet someone and exchange business cards, you are building your contact list.

36. DO SOME "LEARNING CURVE" WORK AT HOME

I once—briefly—hired someone to work for my company as an independent contractor. He proceeded to charge us for the time he spent learning about our business and reading our publications. He lasted about a month, until I discovered all the things I was paying for that should not have been charged to me.

If you want to (1) get ahead at work and (2) make yourself a more valuable employee, take it upon yourself to learn as much as you can about your job, your employer, and your industry ... on your own time. While it is acceptable in most organizations to do some of this during your first few days on the job, make sure you limit it. Take literature and pertinent online information home with you and study it there.

37. HOLD YOURSELF TO A HIGHER STANDARD

There are certain expectations that go with every job. Some are obvious. Some are tacit. Regardless, you will be expected to meet them.

In most organizations, there is zero tolerance for crossing the line of propriety and good behavior. Make sure your behavior is not just good, but unimpeachable. Don't cut yourself any slack on this point. If you do, you may discover that you are not as indispensable as you think you are.

One thing you can do is identify the organization's superstars and analyze what gives them that exalted status. By superstar, I do not just mean the top performers. You will also want to zero in on the really nice, decent, good people who work there. You will frequently find that the true superstars combine both performance and civility.

If they do not, create your ideal out of the traits of different colleagues whom you want to emulate. Then, incorporate them into your own persona.

38. GET TO KNOW YOUR COLLEAGUES

When I arrived at my permanent Army unit in Germany, no one introduced me to anyone else in my platoon. In addition to being genuinely interested in who my colleagues were, I made it a point during breaks in the workday to make the rounds and introduce myself to all 40 or so of my platoon-mates. I quickly learned about their backgrounds, how they wound up in our nuclear weapons unit, their post-Army aspirations, etc. I also offered my assistance with anything that might come up. This accumulated knowledge paid off hugely for me during my tenure in the platoon, in the form of invitations for meals at the homes of married soldiers who lived off post and opportunities to travel around Germany with colleagues who had cars. I also received the best assignments, a good bit of time off from work to pursue some personal interests, coverage when I needed it from the officers, NCOs, and my enlisted peers, and much more. One of my new friends even gave me a bicycle within a week of making his acquaintance.

If no one takes it upon himself or herself to introduce you to everyone in the office, do it yourself. Don't take that omission personally.

If it is apparent that they have a few minutes for small talk, take advantage of it. If not, bide your time.

Above all, get to know their names as soon as possible, then use their names all the time. Developing a reputation for friendliness and interest in others goes a long way toward firmly fitting into the organization.

39. RESPECT THE SUPPORT STAFF

I learned this immensely valuable lesson in my first professional office job, a summer internship with the city manager's office in Rochester, New York. During my first week, upon finishing a draft report on city building engineer staffing levels, I cavalierly wandered over to the executive secretary's desk and flung my handwritten draft into her inbox, accompanied by the flippant comment that I would like to see the finished, typed product on my desk by close of business that day.

If looks could kill, I would have been a dead man. Deservedly so.

Fortunately, the executive secretary was a compassionate lady who knew a greenhorn office worker when she saw one. She asked me if I would take a walk with her down the hall, during which she not so gently lectured me on the proper etiquette governing relations between college-boy interns and permanent staff secretaries.

It was a lesson I took very much to heart. Henceforth, having learned which side the institutional bread was buttered on, I made it a point, nay gospel, to nurture friendships with the secretaries and administrative staff everywhere I went.

In contrast, most of my colleagues everywhere I worked would dump chaotic sheaves of paper on the secretaries' desks and demand finished products by close of business, while making the support staff know in no uncertain terms where they stood in the organizational pecking order.

If you treat the secretaries and receptionists, file clerks, mail-room staff, cleaning crew, et al. with courtesy and respect, the rewards will be considerable. In the pre-computer age, secretaries did all the document preparation. I was invariably first in line for their help (until that uncomfortable yet fortuitous walk down the hall), despite my low- and subsequently mid-level rank and notwithstanding their other priorities. The reasons were probably because (1) I took the time to say hello every day and ask them about their lives; (2) I remembered their birthdays with cards and small presents; (3) from time to time I brought them small desserts and other items (always remember that "desserts" is "stressed" spelled backward); (4) the work I asked them to do for me was always neat, readable, and well organized; and (5) I always thanked them for their efforts on my behalf.

By the way, Godiva chocolates never fail.

40. REMEMBER NAMES AND PERSONAL INFORMATION

When you meet people in your organization, make it a point to lock in their names and any personal information they share with you, such as whether they are married or single, their children, their leisure activities, etc. Until this becomes second nature to you, consider keeping a private notebook in which you can write down this information while it is still fresh in your mind.

This is what Bill Clinton did from the time he was in diapers and decided he might enjoy being president one day. By the time he threw his hat in the ring, he had amassed file cards on over 30,000 individuals with whom he had come in contact during his life, according to his biographers. While I am not suggesting behavior quite as obsessive-compulsive as this, a modified version is not a bad idea.

41. HITCH YOUR WAGON TO A CONSTELLATION (NOT JUST ONE STAR)

Cultivate mentors (plural). It is always a good idea to have more than one "rabbi" within an organization. Why limit yourself? Why not seek out all the help you can get? Moreover, it may be dangerous to invest too much capital in a single individual who suddenly falls out of favor and is either shunned or worse, gone.

Be a disciple. You will learn a lot and you will gain some protection against the vagaries of organizational politics and arbitrariness. Everyone loves and is flattered by a mentoring role. Seek them out.

A young friend of mine works for a venture capital fund that is suffering mightily from the great financial meltdown. Although he was one of the last people hired by the fund, he is still there, a minor miracle considering that there have been three mass layoffs of comparable professionals in just six months.

How has he managed to survive? First, by taking his work seriously and working hard. Second, by being blessed with an unusually engaging personality. People naturally like him and gravitate to him. But more important, by hitching himself to the senior people that he admires and by volunteering to do work for them during slowdowns in his own assignments.

Just be careful whom you select to perform this role for you. Make sure your mentors have a good reputation and strong credibility with their own bosses.

42. AVOID ANSWERING TO MORE THAN ONE SUPERVISOR

One of my early career-counseling clients found himself in the terrible position of being competed over by two supervisors, each of whom expected a full day's work out of him. Worse, since his law firm expected its young associates to put in more than a

40-hour week anyway, my client found himself working 100-hour weeks in a futile attempt to satisfy the unreasonable demands of two masters. This had been going on for over a year before he sought me out.

Worse, this untenable situation was turning his home life into a wreck. His wife threatened him with divorce if he did not resolve the situation and said that she would move back home to Utah with his toddler.

It was not easy to extricate my client from this situation, but eventually we succeeded (once he got up the gumption to confront both puppet masters simultaneously and ask them to sort his work time out between them). It would have been much easier to nip the matter in the bud before it escalated and locked itself in as a permanent condition.

If you sense that this may be about to happen to you, do not permit it. Sit down with both competing supervisors simultaneously and ask them to devise a solution satisfactory to all parties with respect to the apportionment of your time. Assuming the two bosses are coequals, the Solomonic solution—dividing your time in half—may be the best one. If they still do not see the wisdom and logic of your proposal, take the matter to a higher authority and ask that person to decide for whom you should be working.

43. BE A TRENDS ANALYST

This is one of the more important principles in this book.

Study trends in your practice areas, your industry and employment sector, and across the national and world economies. The more you know about how and where things are going, the better you will be able to understand where you might fit into the big picture, not to mention where the big picture is moving.

Not only will trends analysis alert you to opportunity, it will also help you identify potential dangers to your job security. What you want to develop is an *early warning system* so that you will have time to plan your next move.

Read the commercial legal journals, bar journals, and trade journals for your industry, as well as a good national daily newspaper (e.g., *New York Times, Washington Post, Philadelphia Inquirer*) and weekly news magazine (e.g., *Newsweek, Time, U.S. News and World Report, The Economist*), plus at least one good business journal (e.g., *Wall Street Journal, Financial Times, Investors Business Daily.*) Being an attorney, you may not have time for all of this, but you can certainly keep up with the major news and business stories on these publications' websites.

When you read them, do so with a critical eye. Don't take everything you see in print or online as gospel. Remember, the people who put these publications together do so under rigorous deadlines, so they tend to jump to conclusions and miss things. Moreover, they all have a point of view, regardless of what they might profess about journalistic neutrality and lack of bias.

Filter everything you learn through your own experience and your need to know what the future portends. Ask yourself: how does this trend affect me and my organization? Discuss these vital issues with your spouse, friends, and colleagues.

If you watch TV news, keep in mind that the words contained in an entire half-hour newscast fit comfortably on the front page of a newspaper, with room left over. If you have to rely on broadcast news for much of your information, try to listen to National Public Radio or watch *The News Hour* on public television; these delve a bit deeper than commercial networks and stations.

Absorb as much solid information as you can. Be an information sponge. We live in a time when information is power. Be greedy for it. Just make sure you get it from credible sources.

Anticipating the future may be one of the most important uses of your time. Just ask the manufacturers, distributors, and maintainers of gas lighting in the late 19th century or the American fishing industry today. They didn't think very much about the future, and boy did it hurt. Ask any chronically out-of-work cod fisherman in Gloucester, Massachusetts, about his future. It will not be a promising tale.

44. DON'T BECOME DAZZLED BY FADS

Fads are no substitute for common sense or hard work pursuant to a well-thought-out plan. Total quality management, employee empowerment, team building, reinventing government, reengineering the corporation, rightsizing . . . These are great titles for books, but that appears to be all they are. They were *the* hot management mantras only a few years ago. Does anyone remember them? Or what they were all about?

The bottom line is still . . . the bottom line. If that were not the case, how come all of this obsessive worship of frankly meaningless buzzwords has not substantially increased law firm or corporate profits or economic growth?

Organizations become enthusiastic—often breathless—about vague concepts like these that can be distilled into one or two pithy words or an alliterative phrase, but which are usually devoid of substance and soon to pass (quite properly) into the black hole of history. Who remembers zero-based budgeting or supply-side economics, for example? Like a bad dream, we have fortunately forgotten the amount of wasted time, money, and energy expended by law firms, corporate in-house counsel offices, and government general counsel offices—not to mention millions of gallons of media ink and TV talking head appearances—on these fleeting and mercifully debunked notions.

Of course, you probably will find yourself at some point in your career in an organization temporarily enamored of and obsessed with the management fad of the moment. In this case, you may have to "go along in order to get along" until the organization comes to its senses. Don't let it get you down. Eventually, even the most gullible outfits come to their senses. Pretend it's *The Emperor's New Clothes* and that you are the only person who can see that the emperor is as naked as a plucked chicken. Just don't say it out loud. Give it the lip service it is due and nothing more. Eventually, your colleagues will wake up and sanity will return.

For all the hoopla about these purported new approaches to business and management, the old-time virtues are still what really make the difference. Hard work. Thoughtfulness. And a good attitude.

45. BE AN "INTRAPRENEUR"

An intrapreneur is nothing more than an entrepreneur who is not self-employed, but rather works for someone else and waxes entrepreneurial within that context. Every organizational lawyer can—and should—think like an entrepreneur and become an intrapreneur.

Looking at yourself as someone who is self-employed pays a lot of benefits over the long haul. It enables you to focus on what is really important to your organization. It forces you to be innovative and creative. It nurtures self-reliance. It may even help you on the outside, should you ever decide to open your own practice. And it makes for a very compelling résumé when you want to change jobs.

It also means you will not (like so many of your colleagues) rely on your bosses to manage your legal career for you. You will be intelligent enough—and develop sufficient experience, skills, and self-assurance—to take the necessary steps to manage your own destiny. An intrapreneur naturally attends to his or her own personal and professional development.

An intrapreneur is also someone who asks himself or herself who the clients are and what will make them stay with your firm or company—and engage your organization for additional legal services—then acts accordingly.

Finally, an intrapreneur is a leader, someone who does not wait for events to wash over him or her, but who acts proactively to control those events.

46. ADD VALUE

You simply cannot go wrong if you filter everything you do through the question: am I adding value? People who think in terms of adding value to existing products and services are the ones who will advance and who will be the last ones to turn out the lights in the unfortunate event your employer downsizes or has to close its doors.

You don't have to be working in a law firm or corporation in order to add value. You might work for a gorvernment office. The function of government at all levels is essentially the same: to provide the market (voters and taxpayers) with goods and services. Instead of voting with their dollars, the consumers of government goods and services vote with their votes.

No matter where you work or what you do, you are in a good position to analyze your function, your organization's products, services, and processes, etc., and to find ways to improve or add value to them. For example, one of my company's publications was a legal jobs bulletin (which evolved into the *www.AttorneyJobs.com* website). We added value to it by providing special application forms for the positions in the bulletin that required them. We did not directly make money on this value-added transaction, but we earned the respect and loyalty of many of our customers because we gave them an added value. We gave them a convenient way to "one-stop shop" for a variety of forms that, were they to search for them individually, would have cost them a good deal of time, effort, and money (not to mention frustration since government—the generator of many of these forms—is not exactly rapid-response oriented).

Similarly, we developed a kit that helped attorney job candidates complete a rather complex and widely used U.S. government employment application form. Purchasers of this kit were also offered the opportunity to obtain up to one hour of professional career counseling at half of our customary rate. The half-price offer added value to the kit and became a new revenue center for the business.

You can do this with almost anything. Just visit your nearest McDonald's to see how this is done at a very simple—yet sophisticated—level. McDonald's constantly changes its product mix after obtaining considerable feedback from its market research.

If you are a corporate lawyer in a publicly traded company, your constant question should be: how can I contribute to increasing shareholder value? If you work for a law firm, the question would be: how can I maintain current clients and garner new ones? If you work for a government legal office, you might ask: how can I improve legal services to my internal clients and my agency's services to the public? Also, how can I save the taxpayer money?

47. ADAPT

In order to survive—and succeed—in the 21st-century workplace, you must be adaptable. Change is now a constant. Sudden change, as we tragically learned on September 11, 2001, and recently with the acknowledgement of the global financial meltdown, is now a fact of life. Resisting change is futile—a complete waste of your time. It is also illogical . . . and *very* dangerous.

Equally important, the *pace* of change is accelerating. The life cycle of a computer chip is a perfect example. The "286" lasted around four years, the "386" two years, and the "486" one year. The "486" was replaced by the Pentium chip and within a year by the Pentium II chip. Almost as soon as the advent of the Pentium II was announced, a competing announcement of a dramatic new chip technology caused the price of Intel stock to plummet.

Netscape, one of the hottest of the new technology companies that rode the early Internet wave, came up with new versions of its Navigator software browser *every three months!* As if that was not enough to keep pace, Netscape discovered that, in order to compete with Microsoft's Internet Explorer, *it had to give away Navigator for free!*

In addition to adapting to change—and being eager to try new ways of doing things—you will have to demonstrate an equivalent eagerness to factor in the pace of change by showing not only enthusiasm for something new, but also the ability to change course instantly.

Technology alone is already radically changing the way legal—and every other—business is done. Computers, fax machines, cellular telephones, iPhones, beepers, networks, online services, PDAs, MP3s, voice organizers, laser printers, teleconferencing, color copiers, scanners, and many other stunning innovations are altering the way we work all the time. And as technological refinements and upgrades charge into the workplace, we hardly have time to learn one new system or way of doing things before it is superseded!

In addition to becoming adaptable to change in your work environment, you must also adapt to the diverse people with whom you will work. Thanks to the turmoil wrought by economic uncertainty, the globalization of the economy, the increasing mobility of the population, and the loosening of laws formerly restricting business combinations, you will find yourself working with a much greater variety of very different people. These people may be replete with idiosyncrasies, annoying personal habits, erratic behavior, strange clothing, and downright weirdness. If you are so rigid and stiff that you cannot accommodate or abide all of this stuff, you better find a job that enables you to operate as a hermit.

Inflexibility in the workplace is virtually a guarantee of a pink slip.

48. SOLVE PROBLEMS . . . DON'T CREATE THEM

Developing a reputation as a problem solver is the gold standard of job security. One of my law firm clients had to lay off a number of associates due to the loss of a major corporate client. The firm sent me the résumés of the associates to be terminated, and I immediately noticed that one résumé stood out: a woman who described herself as the go-to person in the firm's securities practice whenever a new issue or case of first impression arose. She included an addendum to her résumé that described one such occurrence in detail. I was impressed and called the firm's managing partner and asked her if the firm had included this particular résumé in error. When I read her what was contained in the résumé addendum, the managing partner remembered a similar episode when she had gone to this attorney with a new issue. She immediately pulled the résumé from the group to be laid off.

In contrast, lawyers who create problems—or resist solving them—for their employers are likely to be the first to go. A downsizing is an opportunity for a legal office to divest itself of problem employees. In these economic times, being labeled a problem employee is dangerous to say the least.

49. HIT A HOME RUN WITH YOUR FIRST ASSIGNMENT

Throw yourself into your first task body and soul. Go the extra mile. Knock your boss's socks off with your performance. Do whatever it takes to dazzle.

How you perform on your first assignment will *set the tone* for how you are perceived and will create a lasting organizational impression. Take advantage of this opportunity to make them think you are a superstar.

My first assignment at the Defense Department was to analyze the application of certain laws to U.S. territories and possessions. It was apparent that, while of some policy significance, this was not exactly my superiors' highest priority. Nevertheless, I threw myself into the task with enthusiasm, worked late and on weekends, and drafted a report that went quite a ways beyond what was expected. It not only examined the set of laws in question, but also predicted how future legislation might be subjected to the same tests the courts had devised for determining the extent of applicability of law in U.S. territories and possessions outside the 50 states and the District of Columbia.

My analysis not only gained immediate praise from my supervisors, but it also provided me with two additional benefits:

1. Instant credibility, which resulted in much more important assignments
2. Considerable autonomy with respect to both projects and workplace flexibility

You will never have a better opportunity to make a great—and lasting—impression than when you first begin work.

50. TREAT EVERY ASSIGNMENT AS IMPORTANT

The advice above about hitting a home run with your first assignment does not mean to imply that you can slack off thereafter into bunt-single territory. On the contrary, once you have impressed your bosses with your initial competence, the expectations they have about you will be stratospheric. Don't disappoint them. Every task you are given is important to someone in the organization's hierarchy. Take them all seriously and perform each of them with care and dispatch.

Chapter 3

Securing Your Status

*C*HAPTER 3 IS THE LONGEST *and probably the most important component of this book because it is where most of the lawyers I have counseled fall down. It demonstrates how to build upon the foundation the employee has constructed by virtue of applying the principles described in chapters 1 and 2. Chapter 3 discusses how to lock in the indispensability factor. The underlying theme is that this is no time to relax and rest upon your initial laurels.*

Instead, this is the time to make sure you are prepared to make a terrific continuing impression on your new bosses and colleagues.

This is where you prove your worth to the organization, spread your wings, make yourself an invaluable contributor, and develop the kind of relationship with your bosses that makes them conclude that they cannot afford to lose you.

It is not enough to go to work every day, do the minimum expected of you, and go home at night. This is the 21st-century workplace and the rules have changed. There is no such thing anymore as "lifetime employment." You can be here today, gone tomorrow, and unemployed with no prospects whatsoever the day after. But you can protect against much of that worst-case scenario by adopting and applying these few simple suggestions.

51. FOCUS ON YOUR CURRENT JOB

My first boss when I was fresh out of law school was an inspiration in many ways. Chief among these was his philosophy of work. Simply put, it was the following:

> *"You can make something positive out of any job,*
> *and if you do, great things will happen to your career."*

I have advised numerous legal career transition clients using precisely this language. Some of them took it to heart; others did not. The former group did quite well, careerwise. With few exceptions, the latter group did not.

There are two reasons for concentrating your attention and energy on your current job:

1. You owe it to your employer to do the best job you can.
2. You owe it to your future to make the most out of each job you hold.

There is never any excuse for giving less than your all to a job. I do not mean by this that you need to be on the job, or even think about it, 24/7. What I do mean is that you need to devote your full attention to it when you are at work and when you take work home. If you are frequently distracted by where you want to go next, you will not do the kind of job of which you are capable. That will hurt the business . . . and it will hurt you.

Concentrating on the job before you does not mean that you should not develop a contingency plan if things do not work out for you in your current position. There may be many reasons why your current job turns sour through no fault of your own. Law is an ever-evolving discipline, never more so than at present. Certain evolutionary changes can have a devastating impact on job security.

It also does not mean that you should file your résumé away and not look at it again until you need it. It is always a sound idea to keep your résumé continually up-to-date.

52. BE COST CONSCIOUS

Cost cutting has become a religion in companies. You can do yourself a lot of good by demonstrating your commitment to cutting costs, looking for waste, and recommending ways to do more for less.

Consider Angela, a mid-level attorney working for a large U.S. government department. Every year her department was required to submit over 100 annual reports to Congress on various programs that it administered. Over the years, the reports had become more and more elaborate documents, sometimes running to hundreds of pages, replete with expensive graphics and other bells and whistles. The increase in expense for producing these reports was inversely proportional to the amount of time members of Congress or their staffs actually spent reading and considering them. In other words, they would arrive on Capitol Hill and immediately be filed away or discarded.

Angela examined the costs of producing these reports and also contacted Hill committee staffers to determine what they did with them when they were delivered. Then she drafted specific recommendations, including drastically downsizing them and deleting all the graphics and assorted bells and whistles. Surprisingly for a government agency, the department accepted and adopted her recommendations with respect to a number of the reports and saved itself and the taxpayers several million dollars.

Several months later there was a reduction in force in Angela's department. When her bosses sat down to determine which employees would be let go, the first decision they made was that they could not afford to lose Angela. She was exempt from the RIF.

53. DEVELOP A PLAN

One of the first things you should do when you begin work is to start constructing your own business and marketing plan for how you are going to succeed in the new position. Think of your plan as:

- A strategy for success
- A means of measuring your progress
- A way to keep you focused on what is important
- A tool for self-discipline

A good way to do this is to follow a typical business and marketing plan model, which usually contains the following elements, modified to reflect that this is a personal—not an organizational—plan:

Position Analysis
- Strategic overview of your position
- How your position is organized
- The duties and responsibilities of your position
- How your qualifications match up against these duties and responsibilities

Competitive Analysis

- Who are you directly competing with in the organization?
- Who are you indirectly competing with in the organization?
- What are these individuals' competitive advantages (strengths) and disadvantages (weaknesses)?

Customer and Client Analysis

- Who are your customers (e.g., partners, senior counsel, practice area leaders, line units, etc.) and clients?
- What are their legal needs?
- What legal services and/or expertise will satisfy these needs?

Marketing Plan

This section should outline your strategy for success, i.e., for making yourself indispensable.

Key components:

- Description of your desired strategic position
- Detailed descriptions of your service offerings—and potential service extensions
- Descriptions of your desired image and branding strategy
- Descriptions of your proposed indispensability strategies, e.g.:
  - Contacts
  - Indispensability initiatives
    - Becoming the go-to employee for specific matters
    - Developing unique knowledge and expertise
  - Blog potential
  - Referral services

- ○ Specialty certification (not possible in all states)
- ○ Memberships
- ○ Seminars you could offer
- ○ Teaching CLE
- ○ Writing for publication
- ○ Current and potential strategic marketing partnerships/alliances

Appendix
- Step-by-step checklist of how you will execute the plan
- Timeline

Your plan will never be a finished document. Rather, consider it an ever-changing road map to job success that you will review and adjust periodically.

54. HAVE A VISION

A worldview is a positive thing to develop as you go through life. It is much more than a superficial political ideology. It is more of an ideal, something you can aspire to, something to give you a *framework*, a frame of reference, an order to your existence, and something bigger than yourself and your immediate surroundings.

The Germans, who have a unique talent for coining words to describe the indescribable (and then capitalizing them to demonstrate how truly important they are), call this a *Weltanschauung*.

Occasionally, a fortunate few get to put their ideas about how the world should behave and look into practice. Adolph Hitler did. Joseph Stalin did. You may not agree with their worldviews, but they certainly developed that concept to the fullest. So did George Washington, Thomas Jefferson, Abraham Lincoln, Franklin Roosevelt, and Ronald Reagan.

A vision gives you both goals and a structure into which to fit the things you do to achieve those goals. If they don't fit easily, maybe that is a sign that you should not be forcing them, or even wasting time on them. It also provides you with objectives that will help you plan each day at work, forcing you to focus on what is important and to triage what is not. That, in turn, will translate into a purposeful work ethic that not only keeps you directed, but impresses others as well.

55. STUDY THE COMPETITION

It is critically important to know your competition and adjust your strategic planning accordingly. When it comes to your job and career, "competitive intelligence" can mean the difference between climbing the ladder of success and falling into a career abyss.

Attorneys need to know the competition on three levels:

1. Internal competition. This includes all of your attorney colleagues and others who are competing with you for (1) attention, (2) promotions, and (3) survival.

Recent statistics on making partner in a law firm are very unfavorable. Only around 9 percent of each associate class makes partner at the firm where they began their legal careers. In a down economy, partnership quickly becomes an even more unattainable goal.

Rising to the top of a corporate counsel office is becoming equally difficult. Fortune 500 corporations are no longer the engines of legal job creation they used to be. Technology, the rise of paralegals, mergers and acquisitions, outsourcing (Indian attorneys in Mumbai and Bangalore, for example, are increasingly being employed by the major U.S. legal research organizations), globalization, and the Great Recession have all contributed to this new paradigm.

Bank counsel offices are a good example. The 1990 recession and the collapse of the savings and loan industry forced banks to find ways to save on personnel costs. They discovered that they could do without so many in-house lawyers and adopted a new (unwritten) formula: $500 million in assets = one attorney. The prior formula was $50 million in assets = one attorney.

Fewer corporate lawyers means fewer opportunities to advance within the organization. It also means less turnover.

Even government law offices are competitive. Government lawyers compete for promotions and good assignments just like their counterparts elsewhere. While there may be more job security, it is just as easy to be overlooked and bypassed for promotion in government as anywhere else.

Moreover, some government law offices are even more competitive than the private sector because they actually measure attorney performance. Trademark attorneys at the U.S. Patent and Trademark Office work under a production quota system where they are expected to process a certain number of trademark applications each year. Attorneys who exceed the quota can earn bonuses and receive favorable consideration for promotion. Those who fall below the quota risk losing their jobs during any reductions in force.

Regardless of where you work, you need to know who your competition is, as well as your relative strengths and weaknesses compared to your competitors. Who gets the choice assignments? Why? Who has the best mentors? Who works hardest? Who works most efficiently? What makes them productive? Who are the client development stars? What makes them successful at it? Who makes partner? Why?

Once you gather this intelligence, you need to determine what you have to do to beat the competition.

2. External competition—attorneys. You need to be constantly aware of legal demographics in general and legal hiring trends in particular. Thirty-five years ago, the U.S. lawyer population was 250,000.

Today, it is almost 1.2 million, a much faster growth rate than U.S. population. Add 40,000+ new graduates from American Bar Association (ABA)–approved law schools, plus thousands more from non-ABA law schools, and you see the problem: too many lawyers chasing too few mainstream jobs.

Another factor is increasing the competitive pressure on the profession: the Great Recession is prompting an increase in law school applications from two sources: (1) individuals deferring their job searches until the economy improves and (2) financial services professionals and MBAs seeking better career outcomes.

Competitive intelligence concerning the large number of attorneys out there should not be limited to general legal market demographic information. It should also include legal hiring—and firing—trends. If major law firms and corporations lay off attorneys in droves (as they have been in 2008 and 2009), you know that you will have a lot of competition from a large number of very exceptional lawyers with outstanding résumés. In just one January day in 2009, U.S. companies laid off over 70,000 employees, including many attorneys. Times like that are not propitious for job seekers. That fact alone tells you that you need to upgrade your indispensability strategy.

3. External competition—rival businesses. Intelligence gathering should also include your employer's competitors. Knowledge of your organization's competitors is a necessary business fact of life, especially in an e-commerce environment where websites, product offerings and substitutions, strategic alliances, etc. are constantly evolving. Not being up on the competition is a surefire way to jeopardize your job.

Understanding the competition is a given in the private sector. It is just as essential in the government. When I was at the new U.S. Department of Energy in the late 1970s, one of the first things I did was read the Department of Energy Authorization Act, the law that established the department. I discovered that the act also gave the Departments of Interior, Defense, and Justice, and the Nuclear Regulatory Commission, Federal Trade Commission, and Environmental Protection Agency large slices of the energy pie. Consequently, I kept up with developments at these "rival" agencies, a habit that proved very valuable on many occasions.

Every organization—private, public, and nonprofit—is selling something. Global Amalgamated sells widgets, along with umpteen other companies. The House Ways and Means Committee sells health-care policy and legislation, along with at least eight other House committees. The American Heart Association wants your contribution. So do a host of other presumably well-meaning charitable institutions.

The more you learn about the competition, the better you will be able to *anticipate* their future moves, defend against them, and perhaps help your employer *leapfrog* over them. Study the competitors' annual reports, do a periodic search for articles about them, learn what they do and to whom they do it. Analyze the differences between their operations and yours.

You also need to be concerned about organizational competitors in order to:

- Develop an *early warning sensitivity* about any pending layoffs so that you can accelerate your business and marketing plan and institute defensive measures
- Look for *ideas and best practices that you can promote* in order to keep your employer's business viable and, ideally, growing

Here is an example of how an early warning system might work: You work in your firm's securitization practice. Your intelligence network tells you that law firms are laying off securitization attorneys due to the collapse of the mortgage lending market and the bad name that securitized mortgages have earned with politicians and the public. You conclude that it might only be a matter of time—and a short time at that—before layoff fever hits your law firm.

Consequently, you know that you need to take steps to protect your job. You examine your transferable knowledge and skills carefully and identify several that other firm practice areas might also value: ability to understand complex financial documents, negotiating ability and experience, and transactional document drafting skills. You then recast your résumé to reflect those skills and begin a campaign to cultivate the relevant practice leaders.

56. THINK GLOBALLY

In staying current, expand your research and learning beyond U.S. borders. The transportation, telecommunications, and financial revolutions are proceeding so rapidly that you can no longer afford to think of yourself, your position in the greater competitive scheme, or your organization only in national terms. This is especially true of law firms and corporations.

The world is not becoming a smaller place. It already is one. It is just as easy to move capital from Manila to Miami as it is to move it from Fort Lauderdale to Miami. It is rapidly becoming almost as easy for companies to find labor anywhere in the world, and probably cheaper labor than you. Just look what is happening in the professional legal research community, with more and more Indian attorneys replacing American attorneys.

This outsourcing development has shocked the legal community and has broad implications for other legal arenas. It may soon affect a much broader universe of lawyers. Any practice area or component that is largely document-based may find its work leaving these shores for less expensive common-law jurisdictions. It is not only blue-collar workers who will suffer from how easy it has become for companies to move around the globe in order to identify and enlist cheap labor. In the "knowledge era," this can be accomplished electronically and instantaneously.

Do not assume that your only competition is from Americans. Factor a routine study of global legal and business trends into your career management efforts.

57. PLAY TO WIN

Vince Lombardi, the legendary coach of the world champion Green Bay Packers, once said: "Winning isn't everything. It's the only thing."

That is as true of the working world as it is of the world of sports. Just ask any of the losers.

In the ideal world of fantasies and fairy tales and kids' much-too-early exposure to organized athletics, not to mention grading in school, "participation" is the new political correctness. Winning and losing, parents and kids are told, are not important. Hogwash. Don't believe this for a minute. The world does not work that way at all. It never has. It never will. So get used to reality.

This does not mean you cannot play fair or hard or that there is not a right way and a wrong way to go about competing. There is. Even boxing, that most brutal of blood sports, where death can reside in the next punch, has its rigorous rules of combat. Even war has a body of law (often violated). Naturally, business and work do, too. These standards of conduct should be observed. But don't let anyone delude you for a moment that *trying* is the end-all. *Winning* is what it is all about.

58. IDENTIFY AND COMMAND THE "CHOKE POINTS"

If the title of this section sounds like it was lifted from Alfred Thayer Mahan's 19th-century treatises on naval strategy, good.

Historically, the strategic military concept of the choke point has proven determinative of many, if not most, of the major conflicts between nations: the Greeks at the pass of Thermopylae, where a handful of Spartans held up the massive Persian army long enough to give the Athenians time to gather themselves for the final naval confrontation off Salamis; the Japanese sweep into Malaya, Singapore, and Indonesia at the beginning of World War II in order to control the Malaccan Straits; the German attempts to take control of the Suez Canal and Gibraltar in World War II; Gallipoli in World War I; the pre-positioning of tactical nuclear weapons in the Hof and Fulda Gaps along the Iron Curtain during the Cold War; the overwhelming naval force sent to the Persian Gulf during Desert Storm. All of these were attempts to control the choke points, the key strategic locations where battles and nations and glory are won and lost.

Choke points are not only strategic geographic features that nations and armies struggle over during wars. They also exist in every organization. If you are the only one who knows how to operate a new technology that has the potential for becoming central to the organization, or are the go-to attorney for expertise and strategic advice on financial regulatory law, you are in a commanding position with regard to a choke point.

Identifying the choke points and then positioning yourself to control them—becoming the gatekeeper—will put you in a unique position. If you are successful in doing this, you will probably be the last one out the door, the one responsible for turning out the lights, in the unlikely event the whole organization collapses.

Examine your organization's processes and systems in order to pinpoint the choke points. Then, learn as much as you can about them: how they work, their problems, possible solutions. Use your downtime to familiarize yourself with them, and you will have done some fancy pre-positioning yourself!

59. SEEK SYNERGIES

Sometimes the obvious is right in front of our eyes, and therefore difficult to spot. You have to back up to see it. And then you feel a bit foolish for overlooking it previously.

The best example of this is a short course soldiers usually get in boot camp. The course is designed to teach reconnoitering and surveillance. The trainee stands on a rampart and is supposed to spot an enemy sapper somewhere out in front of him or her. The natural tendency of almost every soldier among the millions who have gone through basic training in the military is to squint and look out as far as the eye can see in order to pinpoint the hostile infiltrator. Invariably, the enemy trooper is lurking only a few feet away, right in front of the spotter and unseen by him or her.

It is a powerful lesson, one not easily forgotten by those of us who have been embarrassed—and shaken—by our recklessness.

Synergies are all around us. For years, my company published a large amount of legal career information for attorneys. We had been doing this for almost a decade before it occurred to us that we probably knew more about the legal employment market in the United States, if not the world, than anyone else, including those organizations providing career counseling and outplacement services to lawyers. The question naturally arose: why aren't we providing these services? It was a natural synergy. But it took us years to realize and act upon it.

Synergies are also possible outside an organization. If you publish a DVD on "Everything You Ever Wanted to Know about Widget Manufacturing," you should look around for other things that are available on the same subject before putting your DVD into production. Perhaps the U.S. General Accounting Office has published a recent study on "Government Regulation of the U.S. Widget Industry." You may discover that the Arizona-Mexico Trade Commission has a videotape available on "Retraining Defense Workers to

Become Widget Quality Control Inspectors," or that the American Widget Manufacturers and Distributors Association has issued a computerized directory of Widget-related manufacturing facilities, or that the Department of Commerce has a promotional pamphlet on "Opportunities for Widgeteers under NAFTA and CAFTA." All of these are potentially worthy candidates for inclusion in your DVD product and would make it that much more enticing to the market. The value each of these contributory products could greatly enhance the potential success of your undertaking.

Whenever you contemplate what your organization is doing, think of related elements that could enhance company sales, company service, and your future.

60. ANALYZE SYSTEMS AND SEEK SOLUTIONS

Every work environment has systems—ways of doing something that involve a variety of sequential tasks. There is no system that cannot be improved. That is a big advantage for you as an employee. You can easily study these systems, break them down, ask yourself how to make them better, and develop reasoned suggestions for improving them. If you do that, you will have taken a giant step toward indispensability.

One of my employees once studied how we handled the paper backup of customer orders for our legal publications. We used to do it by month and day. If we received 40 orders on the first of June, they all went into the slot marked "June 1." The problem arose when we had to search the backup in order to resolve a customer service problem. We had to determine when the order was received, then go into the June 1 slot and paw through all the orders until we found the one in question. If anyone was even the slightest bit careless about the order filing date (which happened often), we had to reinvent this cumbersome process for all the days around the presumed order date.

After some study, she made the following suggestion: instead of filing orders by date, why not file them alphabetically, by the customer's last name? It was an excellent idea and immediately made us more efficient. Gone were the filing date problems. All the Zipplewhites and Zygmunts were filed together under Z and the Morrisses and Montagues under M. The system worked great, and our employee got a raise soon after it went into effect.

Every problem cries out for a solution . . . even if no one around you is smart or alert enough to perceive it as a problem.

61. CHALLENGE THE CONVENTIONAL WISDOM

Remember the Shah of Iran? Few people do, but 30 years ago all we heard from Washington was that "the Shah is indispensable," or "Iran without the Shah is unthinkable." Guess what? No Shah. Somehow Iran is still there, a big thorn in the United State's side for three decades, a source of tremendous instability in the Middle East, and a danger to the world.

Had someone thought to challenge this idiotic conventional wisdom in the 1970s, we might all be a lot better off today. But no one did. So a major component of U.S. foreign policy was driven by an absurd premise. Much to our regret.

This kind of stuff goes on all the time in every corner of human activity. Twenty-five years ago, the Big Three U.S. automakers all said, "Americans won't buy fuel-efficient cars." Unfortunately for the millions of autoworkers and employees of auto suppliers and servicing companies who are losing their jobs as a result, someone forgot to tell that to the Japanese and Koreans.

As late as 1977, the president of Digital Equipment Corporation, then the second largest computer company in the world, said, "There is no reason for any individual to have a computer in their home." I guess someone forgot to tell that to Steve Jobs and Steve Wozniak, who tinkered with the idea of the personal computer in a garage and ended up starting Apple. And let's not forget Bill Gates.

There are two ways to challenge conventional wisdom: One is to be obnoxious about it, in which case no one will listen to you. The second way is to be diplomatic about it, in which case you will generally have a better opportunity to have your views aired.

This does not mean that you should go ahead and challenge everything simply for the sake of being a contrarian. Before you attack, make sure you have some credible foundation for your assertions. Once you do, don't be afraid to go for it.

62. IF IT AIN'T BROKE . . . FIX IT ANYWAY!

This is another way of underscoring the points made in the two sections immediately preceding this one. Turn the conventional wisdom on its head.

The world is simply turning over and moving too fast for any of us to sit still. Look at the air travel industry. With deregulation just over 30 years old, the industry has been wrenched inside out. Airlines that were mainstays of American enterprise, household words even, like Braniff, National, PanAm, TWA, and Eastern, are now only distant memories. They thought they could proceed under the new Wild West of deregulation using their old tried and true ways. They couldn't, and a lot of employees and stockholders lost a great deal because of management's ostrich-like bad judgment.

Similarly, energetic start-ups like People's Express, Presidential, and Air Florida were only around long enough to lose a lot of folks their shirts (not to mention their lives). Even the survivors are in some trouble, but at least many of them finally got this message. Southwest Airlines, one of the great innovators and few success stories to come out of airline deregulation, experimented with paperless ticket systems and other innovations in an attempt to corner the market (albeit briefly) on customer convenience and cost cutting. It worked beautifully, and Southwest gained a temporary advantage, which did not last more than a few months because it forced all the other air carriers to follow suit. Interestingly, Southwest's management calculated that its advantage would last only a few months, if that. They were right. This is how fast the world is changing.

To play out the airline example a step further, lets say you are a reservation agent for a Southwest competitor, standing behind a counter at an airport or downtown ticket center, keypunching information into a computer and then printing out a ticket. Maybe you better think about updating your résumé.

And if you think something big, lumbering, and heavy hardware–oriented like airlines are in the throes of rapid change, other industries are even more frenetic. Computers, obviously. Chip makers know they have only a few months, and often only a few weeks, to profit from innovation before they are "reverse engineered," emulated, and leapfrogged by the competition!

Lawyering is also not sacrosanct. The professional collegiality that marked law firm practice is gone, replaced by a highly competitive scramble to retain clients and secure new ones.

The point is, it can happen in any industry, no matter how large or how narrowly cast. Whether it's railroading—an industry with fixed assets and lots of heavy equipment to move around, microsurgical devices so tiny the naked eye can't see the product, or lawyering, you have to think ahead, anticipate, and tinker with everything, even success. Today's success can very easily and quickly turn into tomorrow's obsolete product or service or means of delivery, interesting only to economic historians, but of no concern at all to today's and tomorrow's consumers (the people who really sign your paycheck).

63. TINKER AT THE MARGINS

At first glance, this probably sounds like contrarian advice. Margin tinkerers are traditionally denigrated and viewed with contempt by popular business book writers. However, they are wrong. Every process and procedure that impacts upon your work can be improved, and improving them in any way at all is an easy way to impress the people who count.

Often, a simple suggestion can prove to be a huge time-saver. If you come across a way of doing something that looks slow, unwieldy, or plain idiotic, think about how it could be improved. Small suggestions are generally avidly sought and appreciated. They don't cost much time, money, or effort to institute, and the rewards to the individual making the recommendation can be both immediate and huge, as well as something of a longer-term insurance policy at crunch time.

Little things add up. People remember and reward the tinkerers.

64. BE PROJECT ORIENTED

Redirect your thinking to the achievement of results. Organizations are not about the daily grind. They are about reaching an end result, an outcome. Even litigation firms need to think this way. Delay and dragging cases out for increased billing purposes is not going to satisfy today's more sophisticated and cost-conscious clients.

It is very easy, day to day, for you and everyone else to lose sight of your organization's mission. By keeping the goal in mind and examining how your daily routine contributes to the goal, you will always be a step ahead of your competition, both within the organization and within your industry.

When you begin work, ask questions that are directed toward discovering your employer's objectives. Make sure you have a good understanding of them early on.

65. THINK LONG TERM

This is not quite the same strategy as involving yourself in long-term projects (see principle 121). What I am suggesting here is taking a long-term view, as opposed to getting overly focused on the achievement of short-term results.

The best and most stable organizations (and consequently, work situations) are those that think in terms of 1 year, 5 years, and 10 years out, not those that think short term. The problem with both American big business and big government is that it is worship of the short term that is king, and the long term be damned.

In the world of publicly traded corporations, the future is unfortunately almost never more than three months away, thanks to the requirement to publish quarterly results and the consequent judgment that analysts and shareholders make about performance. U.S. auto manufacturers are an unfortunately classic example of shortsightedness, willing to sacrifice long-term stability and success for short-term gain to the point that they are at risk of disappearing.

In government, the annual budget cycle drives everything else, planning included. What is worse, as soon as one budget is enacted and put into place by the legislature, the executive branch agencies are already well into planning their next year's budget without the benefit of any evaluation of how this year's budget performed!

The only place in America where people have the luxury of thinking long term without a struggle is among privately held companies. They are answerable only to their owners, who usually work in the company and don't have to report to outside persons. It is no coincidence that these companies have been the engine of in-house counsel office growth.

Don't fall prey to this short-term temptation. Historically, those organizations that took a long-term view ended up the big winners.

66. LOOK FOR THE GROWTH POTENTIAL

When selecting the projects you want to focus on, analyze them for their growth potential. If possible, try to avoid those that are so dubious or pie-in-the-sky that your very association with them may run the risk of rendering you questionable or irrelevant, and therefore expendable.

One of my early legal positions was with the U.S. Department of Energy during its (relatively) exciting early days. When I reported for work my first day, I was given a stack of studies, monographs, and other writings and told to come back when I had devised a set of regulations for the U.S. geothermal steam industry.

A week later, once I had developed a remote clue as to what geothermal steam was, I began to get a nagging feeling that what I was doing was not terribly relevant. At that time, the whole geothermal industry consisted of a few thermal vents in California that were being tapped as energy sources by a couple of experimental researchers. Hardly an industry that required much regulation.

I got up enough nerve to express my skepticism about the value of the assignment to my boss. He sent me right back upstairs to my office after a stirring pep talk about U.S. energy security in the event OPEC kept the oil spigot turned off.

His appeal to my patriotism fueled me for about 24 hours, during which I discovered that geothermal steam production would become economically viable only when the price of a barrel of oil went over $100 (approximately $310 in 2009 dollars). Since oil at that time was at an historic high of $30-something a barrel, I had a hard time contemplating the future viability of this cottage industry. When I went to see my boss armed with this new information, he was annoyed, and impatiently explained to me that a team of departmental lawyers and economists with vast experience in this sort of thing was, at that very moment, writing a report to the president and Congress predicting a $100 price level for a barrel of benchmark Saudi Arabian light crude oil in only two more years.

Still skeptical, I completed the assignment. Shortly thereafter, the price of oil began a steady, long-term decline all the way down to $12 a barrel.

I suspect my geothermal regulations are collecting dust in some warehouse somewhere in Washington, much like the lost ark at the end of *Raiders.*

This first experience at the newly constituted Energy Department convinced me that I had to avoid assignments like that in the future. Fortunately, I did, notwithstanding that my job was fairly secure and the immediate need to do things that were relevant and influential and had growth potential was nowhere near as acute as it is today.

The moral of this story is if you have a choice, opt for the one that contains the seeds of future significant growth and fungibility.

Sidenote: I escaped from the Energy Department after only 10 months. Several years later, the job that was being done by approximately 600 people in my section became part of the job description of one person at the Interior Department.

67. SET QUANTIFIABLE GOALS FOR YOURSELF . . . THEN ANNOUNCE THEM

It is very difficult in many legal jobs today to measure performance on less than a practice area or organization-wide basis. Managers and employees in service organizations, for example, make hundreds of small decisions each day that contribute to, or detract from, company performance. But unlike a factory worker in a manufacturing plant, whose productivity can be easily measured, a service organization manager's decisions usually cannot. Downsizing decisions, consequently, are frequently made more on the basis of "feel" than on the basis of quantifiable performance.

Therefore, it is vitally important to establish your own evaluation criteria, which should be objective, quantifiable, verifiable by others, and publicly known to your supervisor(s). If you get into the habit of doing this for yourself, it can become more than merely a protection; it can also have a positive impact on promotion and advancement within the company and the industry, provided you find ways to communicate your achievements to your bosses.

One way to do this is to *share your productivity goals with your employer* and then write a follow-up memo at the end of the performance period tying your accomplishments to the original communication of your goals. Your boss will be impressed not only with your accomplishments, but also with your skill in organizing and communicating them.

Example: You are an attorney in a law firm. You analyze your firm's client development function and conclude that the average firm attorney gives one presentation per year to potential client groups, such as Rotary Club luncheons. Before launching your initiative, you first determine that you can exceed the average performance. Once you are confident of that, you announce your goals to your supervisor. You write a memo stating your intent to make five presentations per year, a reasonable goal considering your workload and the time available to achieve your goal. You advise him or her that you will deliver a report of your results when the measurement period is over. You communicate to your boss each time you schedule a new presentation. Then, when you have quantified your superior performance, you report your results to your boss. You also include information about your overall client development and specific presentation goals for the coming year.

I have yet to observe a legal or other organization where average performance is so phenomenal that beating it is daunting. Usually, you will find that average performance is not all that difficult to exceed. This is especially true in large organizations that, by their very size, are somewhat "arthritic." Government and large companies are classic examples of this kind of ossification.

68. LEARN FROM EACH CLIENT/CUSTOMER

Every client interaction should be a learning experience and educational opportunity that you can use to become both more client driven and better able to serve the next client who comes along.

Clients are an immensely valuable resource and are a mother lode of information to be mined in terms of market research. They will be uninhibited in relating their gripes about your—and your competitors'—products and services. Whether you deal directly with clients or get your client feedback secondhand from your organization's frontline lawyers, this is the kind of information you should seek above all other.

Clients with whom you come into professional contact can also play a very important role in your quest for indispensability. If the time comes when a downsizing is under consideration, an endorsement of you by an internal or external client can be the difference between termination and retention.

69. FOCUS ON EFFICIENCY

There are always at least two ways to perform any task. Before diving into an assignment, think about the most efficient way to perform and complete it. If you need some useful input, seek out more experienced colleagues who have preceded you down this road. They probably will have some useful tips that will make your task easier and a much more pleasant experience.

70. CONCENTRATE ON THE IMPORTANT THINGS

It is easy to get bogged down in minutiae. It happens all the time to almost everyone. It is human nature to become obsessed with the details while losing sight of the big picture. The only way to avoid falling into this trap is to be constantly vigilant.

To accomplish anything meaningful, you have to stick to broad principles. Leave the step-by-step details to others if you are in a position to do that. The old adage about losing sight of the forest because of the trees is right on point. It is awfully easy to fall into that trap, even for very intelligent people. Just ask Bill and Hillary Clinton about it in the context of their disastrous attempt at health-care reform. They completely forgot about the broad principles, got totally mired in rather minor, insignificant details, generated a monstrous 1,000-plus page piece of legislation whose very heft was intimidating, and lost the initiative (and Congress by a landslide in the next election).

No matter what you think of former President Ronald Reagan, he never forgot what he saw as his broad themes: smaller government, lower taxes, and more defense. That was it. The rest was detail work best left to others. And it worked magnificently for him. It can work for you, too.

One simple suggestion: before you leave the office at night, list the things you hope to accomplish the next day on your calendar. Then prioritize the list, giving primacy to the most important tasks. I do this by assigning a 1 to each highest priority item, a 2 to the next priority group, and a 3 to everything else. If I get through all of my 1s during the day, I have a feeling of accomplishment. I don't worry much about the 2s and 3s.

Don't treat every item on your calendar equally. Some tasks are more important than others. One of the reasons job security became a huge problem for President Jimmy Carter when he ran for a second term was because he never learned this lesson. His calendar contained a lot of items and he set a goal every day of slogging his way through each one of them so he could check them off when each was completed. Consequently, if an item on the list was "decide who gets to use the White House tennis court" and the subsequent one was "call Brezhnev on the hotline and implement the SALT II nuclear weapons treaty," the tennis courts came first because this item was ahead of Armageddon on his daily list.

71. SET PRIORITIES . . .
AND CONSTANTLY TRIAGE THEM

This bit of advice goes hand in hand with the preceding item. The only difference is that it calls for a bit more sophistication and subtlety.

It is not only your priorities you should worry about. You also must factor your boss's and the larger organization's priorities into the equation. If you think that finishing the Amalgamated deal is task number one on your list, but you know that your boss is obsessed with the Corrugated deal, guess which one should occupy the number one position on your list?

But that is not where prioritizing ends. Nothing is permanent in this world except change. Therefore, you have to keep abreast of changes external to your organization and how they might affect your work, not to mention the future and fate of your company and its priorities.

There is an Army Civil Affairs Reserve unit in the Washington, D.C., area that, 10 years after the end of the Cold War, was still spending all of its "weekend warrior" training time on mobilization planning for the Cold War! When asked why, the answer was, "Because we have invested so much time and money in this exercise, it seems a shame to waste it." (Note: It was, of course, your tax dollars that were being wasted.)

This army parable also points out another key prioritization concept: you have to be flexible enough to change your priorities rapidly, if they are no longer relevant or in line with reality.

72. TRY TO PICK UP EACH PIECE OF PAPER—AND EMAIL—ONLY ONCE

Notwithstanding the advent of the so-called paperless office, it seems we are inundated by paper more than ever. It is very easy to become buried in errant sheets of paper very quickly.

That can never happen if you make it a point to deal with each piece of paper only once. If you open an envelope, you will be much better off taking whatever action is necessary to dispense with—and dispose of—the mail inside it right away. Otherwise it will just pile up in your inbox and the next time you see it, it may be too late to deal with or even to remember what you need to do with it. That is tremendously inefficient.

Set aside a chunk of time each day to tackle the paper crush.

The same advice applies to emails.

73. DON'T SLIP DEADLINES

Develop a reputation for getting your work done on time. Since so few people actually do, you will shine by comparison.

Work late and on weekends and at home, if necessary; most of the time, provided you have rudimentary organizational skills, it won't be too painful.

Special note: There are certain work situations, often in law firms, where exploitation of young associates is the name of the game. In these unusual and unique settings, working late and on weekends and at home is commonly expected. Don't go into a work situation like this with your eyes closed.

74. ALWAYS BE ON TIME FOR MEETINGS

This is similar to the advice about coming to work on time. If you are going to make yourself famous in your organization, let it be for something exceptional and positive, not because you develop a reputation as a chronic late-comer.

Nothing irritates colleagues and supervisors more than late arrivals to meetings. This has always been true of face-to-face meetings. It is even more annoying when someone is late to a Web-based meeting or conference call. Who, after all, wants to listen to elevator music?

75. GENERATE AN AGENDA

Open-ended meetings are almost always a waste of time. In contrast, an agenda-based meeting usually manages to complete its work more quickly and actually achieve a result.

You will find many organizations where meetings are held absent an agenda. Once you are settled in and have gained some credibility and respect within your office, consider offering to prepare an agenda whenever you encounter an agenda-less meeting. You will establish an important precedent and a very positive routine to be followed henceforth. Moreover, the person who controls the agenda usually has the most influence at the meeting itself.

Be sure to distribute the agenda to all attendees enough in advance to give them an opportunity to study it and prepare for the meeting. Your cover sheet or transmittal email should also request comments on your proposed agenda.

76. DELIVER ON YOUR PROMISES

This is another one of those important areas where first impressions and overall reputation are critical. If you always fall short on your promises or promise much more than you know you can deliver, it may come back to haunt you when the executives are sitting around the table deciding who goes and who stays.

However, if you want to distinguish yourself from your peers right away, this is an interesting tack: promise more and then deliver on that promise. Promising more than is expected will cause your boss and his or her bosses to sit up and take notice. They will, of course, be skeptical, since they have come to expect that grandiose assertions almost never come to pass. Then, when you deliver the goods, boy will they be impressed!

How do you do this? An easy way is to beat a deadline. Most deadlines, by the way, are eminently beatable. If your boss says, "I want the Cayman Islands report on my desk by close of business Friday," get it on his or her desk a day early. Make a habit of exceeding expectations and this will stick in his or her mind.

This is the kind of thing you want to come to mind when tough decisions about downsizing or promotions are made. This is another situation where it is important to realize that if you are going to make yourself memorable in the organization, you want to do it for a positive reason like this, not for a negative one like never meeting a "drop-dead date."

77. ALWAYS DO IT BETTER THE SECOND TIME

Your ability to improve, even on a job well done, never ceases. You can always find a way to make something better the second time around, thanks to having been around the track once already. Whether it is putting on and promoting a seminar, giving a presentation, writing a report, drafting a pleading, taking or defending a deposition, writing a brief, or any other activity, what you learn from experience is invaluable.

The only catch is, you have to be cognizant of what you are doing, rather than merely going through the motions, in order to profit from experience. There are, unfortunately, a surprising number—perhaps a majority—of members of the legal workforce who learn absolutely nothing from having done something once. They make the same mistakes over and over again. This happens at every level and in virtually every legal and human endeavor.

Look no further than the world of politics and government for examples of people who don't learn from experience, as well as those who learn very well. Jack Kennedy learned valuable lessons from the Bay of Pigs debacle and his presidency benefited. Lyndon Johnson never learned the lessons of escalation in Vietnam, and it destroyed his presidency. Richard Nixon, in contrast, was a quick study in defeat (vice president in 1960, governor of California in 1962), coming back from the political dead to become president and then get reelected.

It doesn't even have to be your own experience to learn a valuable object lesson in how not to do something when it comes your turn to try. It may be better, in fact, that you can learn just as much from the failures of others. Despite the example of the French incursion into Southeast Asia, the United States made exactly the same mistake in intervening militarily, an action that caused American society to turn itself inside out, and one from which our nation still might not have fully recovered. And keep in mind that the French debacle in Vietnam was very fresh in the minds of Washington policy makers. It had only happened a few years before our own ill-advised involvement. Nevertheless, we blundered in anyway, with devastating results.

Vietnam proved to be a disaster and contributed significantly to financial and other problems we faced in the 1970s and early 1980s. Now, a generation later, the government made the same mistake again, conducting a preemptive war in Iraq despite the Vietnam lesson. The lessons of history were ignored.

These kinds of lessons are also legion in the business world: Detroit's ostrichlike refusal, for many years, to notice that foreign competition was eating American car makers alive; labor unions' intransigent attitude toward employers who simply could not afford their workers' demands and still see their businesses prosper, much less survive.

It is important, careerwise, to study the lessons of history from both a macro and a micro perspective. Each form of analysis will teach you a great deal about how to conduct yourself and also about how not to behave.

Macro means the big picture. What are the trends in the industry, both domestic and foreign? Are there outside influences to which one has to pay attention? Is this a growth arena or one that is likely to shrink in the next several years? What are the implications of technology for the industry? Are firms going global or trying to insulate themselves from foreign competition?

Micro means what is happening to you and to your employer in the narrow context.

78. DO IT FASTER

Speed kills. These are words to live by for every general manager in every sport, at every level, professional or pseudo-amateur (i.e., college), in America. Whether it is baseball, basketball, football, hockey, or anything else, the race is to the swiftest. Nothing is more devastating or disruptive to the opposition than pure, unadulterated speed. Nowadays, all the smart player personnel types draft for speed first. Everything else is secondary.

The same is true in business. Time is money. But speed is also critically important on another level in this instant communication age: customer convenience. The overriding demand of contemporary consumers is for more and more convenience. As the public finds its time more pressured, it does not want to waste time needlessly—hence the driving engine of greater and greater convenience. If you can do it quicker than your competition, you will probably win the customer. Thus, the definitive reality for all businesses and comparable organizations today is the need to do what they do . . . faster. And then not to rest on their accomplishments, but to find ways to do it even faster yet.

You can find two perfect examples of the demand for more speed in politics and the Internet. The media mavens who devise political ads understand that you have to get the message across quickly. After conducting numerous focus groups in order to study attention spans, it was concluded by the political class in the run-up to the 2004 election that a television political ad should, ideally, be no longer than nine seconds. No, this is not a typo. *Nine seconds!* A sad commentary on the attention span of the American voter.

When you go to a website, how long do you wait for something to load before you give up and move on to the next site? According to the experts, you won't wait more than 10 seconds.

If you can be the one in your organization to devise ways to deliver your product or service faster, you will be earmarked as a "comer," as someone who management will be watching with great and positive interest. So the message is, look for ways to do it faster.

79. PROOFREAD YOUR WORK BEFORE SUBMITTING IT

Virtually every position in today's legal workforce requires not only oral communication, but also the written variety. Therefore, it is critically important to write your pleadings, memoranda of law, briefs, and reports to others in your organization clearly, concisely, and in plain, easily understandable English.

Spell-check programs should take care of most of the obvious problems with written work. But that is not enough. You also have to read your documents over carefully yourself.

One of my attorneys once cited several statutes in a memorandum that was going outside our organization, using the designation "*Pubic* Law No." instead of "*Public* Law No." Regardless of your feelings about the work of Congress, this citation form is not one that you want to see in a public document. Unfortunately, the error survived spell-checking. It also survived any additional proofreading by the drafter, since he did not bother to proofread very carefully.

Resolve never to hand in an assignment that you have not scrutinized with great care first, before letting other eyes see it. Handing in written work that is replete with typographical errors, spelling mistakes, incomprehensible sentences, abysmal syntax, or other grammatical tortures is inexcusable. It leaves a very bad taste in readers' mouths and will make you memorable, if not famous, for all the wrong reasons.

80. SIMPLIFY

This is somewhat related to marginal tinkering (see principle 63). The ultimate goal is the same: to make things easier for you, for your organization, or for your client.

This is a technique that engineers engage in when modeling new products or processes. Over and over, they examine and reexamine what they are modeling in order to reduce it down to its simplest components, its least common denominator.

The 17th-century French philosopher, physicist, and mathematician Blaise Pascal once wrote a letter to a friend that started off like this:

> *"I am sorry that I am writing you a five-page letter.*
> *I did not have time to write you a one-page letter."*

Coming up with simpler ways of doing things is hard work. It is well worth the investment.

One of the underlying causes of the Great Recession of 2008 and beyond was the increasing complexity of the financial instruments the so-called Wall Street geniuses devised that were then sold by CEOs and their sales forces, neither of whom understood what they were selling to equally mystified investors. The world economy did not plummet into meltdown mode when investments were simple and easy to understand.

These engineering techniques can just as appropriately be applied to virtually any legal or other work situation. If you observe what is going on in your organization as a matter of routine, you can come up with ways to make these routines simpler (translate: *easier, quicker, cheaper*). People who are conscious of this technique and apply it are often amply rewarded for their efforts.

81. BE COGNIZANT OF POLITICAL CONSIDERATIONS

Political venues are hardly the only places where politics looms large and often predominates. Every organization is political, with legal organizations and law offices even more so than others.

You absolutely have to be aware of this fundamental truth at all times. Politics surrounds you and is certain to impact on your career. It is best to keep this in the forefront of your thinking from the time you accept a position.

Political savvy includes knowing as much as you can about power relationships between individuals and among groups in your office and larger organization: who is beholden to whom, who likes and dislikes whom, who is sleeping with whom, how you need to behave toward others, etc.

82. TREAT YOUR BOSSES— AND EVERYONE ELSE—WITH RESPECT

Bosses expect respect (even if they do not command it). They invariably feel that they have earned it. It is one of the perks of being a boss. If they don't get it from employees, they tend to think less of them, which is no help at evaluation time. If you conclude that you truly cannot respect your boss, that may be a sufficient reason to consider changing jobs.

The army staff sergeant in charge of my NATO nuclear weapons squad outranked me and my fellow squad members by several grades. Unfortunately, he had a meek personality that hardly commanded respect and more often prompted derision and defiance by the squad. Nevertheless, I always treated him with respect, which was hard to do because of his demeanor and because my squad mates uniformly made fun of him to his face.

When I was confronted by my colleagues as to why I behaved this way toward our squad leader, I pointed out a number of character traits he possessed that merited our respect and even our admiration: his fairness toward us, the fact that he treated us like mature men, his being a loyal family man despite a very difficult wife and two undisciplined kids, his consistency, his sincere efforts to improve himself and his squad's performance. After my little advocacy lecture, I was no longer criticized by my colleagues.

It quickly became clear that the sergeant respected me far more than anyone else in the squad, if not the entire platoon. Consequently, he gave me an unusual amount of autonomy with respect to my job and my life outside of working hours. As long as I did my job and did it well, he did not care what else I did or where I did it.

83. PATTERN YOURSELF AFTER YOUR BOSS'S POSITIVE TRAITS

Imitation really is the sincerest, surest, and safest form of flattery. Study your bosses' habits and adopt the really good ones and also the ones that are the easiest and most logical for you to embrace. Clothes, mannerisms (that are not bizarre), ways of speaking and moving, and ways of dealing with subordinates and superiors all are fair game.

This is not meant to turn you into a fawning sycophant or a boss clone. Remember, there must be some reason why your boss is your boss—perhaps some personality trait, competency, leadership quality, etc. (Unless, of course, daddy is the big boss.) Try to identify it and model yourself on it.

You do not have to adopt the whole package. My first paid job was as a stock boy in a pharmacy in the small town where I grew up. My boss was obsessed with organization and, at the same time, highly erratic when it came to customer service.

Every container in inventory in the store basement was well marked and easy to retrieve. Every item on the store shelves was in its proper place and shelf replacements were immediately made upon any sale.

At the same time, my boss would leave his customers dangling at the counter waiting for him to fill a prescription if the town fire alarm went off. He was a volunteer fireman and took that responsibility much more seriously than he did his customers' assorted ills.

I was much impressed by his organizational prowess and much appalled by his utter lack of customer relations skills. I adopted and incorporated the former into my work life, but most definitely not the latter.

84. ASK YOUR BOSS FOR ADVICE

People who are asked for their help or advice with important matters, are invariably flattered to know that someone thinks enough of them to approach them on these issues. Bosses are no different. And since it is part of their job description to direct and advise their subordinates, they customarily respond quite naturally and positively to such an approach.

Also, every time you come to your supervisor with an important question, the answer to which is directly related to the well-being of your work unit and the company, you underscore your concern for and commitment to the organizational mission.

One word of warning: be prepared for an informed discussion of the issues you bring to the attention of your boss. Do your homework before knocking on the boss's door.

85. DON'T BOTHER YOUR BOSS WITH PETTY ISSUES

The other side of the coin of knocking on the boss's door for counsel is making a pest of yourself over rather insignificant issues. For example, certain employees cannot seem to resist the temptation to give up immediately when they cannot find a certain file on their computer (why they think their boss will be able to locate it for them is beyond my comprehension) or when their computer, for some minor, easily correctable reason, decides to act persnickety and freeze or balk at sending a file to the printer. All your supervisor can do, once he or she has been rousted out of whatever he or she has been doing (and is naturally annoyed by the interruption), is precisely what you yourself could have done: search methodically for the missing file, send the file to the printer again, turn off the computer or printer and turn it on again, etc.

Supervisors remember stuff like this. It is often the first thing that leaps to mind when the CEO orders each unit to make an across-the-board personnel cut.

86. HELP YOUR BOSS SUCCEED

Your job, and sometimes your career, is linked to that of your boss. If your boss looks good, chances are you will look good, too. Reflected glory.

For this to work, good communication between you and your boss is essential. Ask him or her for feedback periodically. Find ways to make your boss's job easier. Educate him or her as to how to best use your talents. Learn his or her idiosyncrasies. Never permit your boss to be surprised by something you have done or did not do.

87. DON'T INTERRUPT

Don't you hate it when someone interrupts you? Of course you do. Now think of all of the opportunities in the workplace for interruptions: staff meetings; negotiations with other organizations, both internal and external; presentations by supervisors and colleagues; etc. The opportunities for interruption are literally unlimited.

Interrupting someone—peer, superior, or subordinate—at work is more than merely bad manners. It is a faux pas of significant proportions. If you make a habit of it (and the people that do it at all are generally the ones for whom it is almost an addiction), you will be remembered for it.

One of my employees was a chronic interrupter. It did not matter if someone was in a meeting, on the telephone, immersed in important work, or helping someone else solve a problem. Regardless of the circumstances, many of which silently screamed out at her "LATER!" she would blunder in and intrude. She just did not get it. While she was good at some aspects of her duties, or at least good enough to permit her to remain with our organization, she never got a raise and never got promoted. In fact, she went through two rather subtle demotions. Meanwhile, other similarly situated employees went up the corporate ladder, leaving her behind. Every time she would come up for review, I could not overcome my annoyance at her boorish behavior.

88. BE A GOOD LISTENER

Developing good listening habits is essential to success in any endeavor. Work is no different. In law, it is crucial. An awful lot of essential information is imparted at work through verbal communication. It is astounding to consider how little of it registers.

For example, I always told new employees, over and over again, to study our products and services and ask questions so that they would become conversant about them and be able to discuss them intelligently with customers and clients. No matter how often I reiterated this request—and the value of doing it—it never seemed to get through. When I would bring it up again, it was as if it were the first time it had ever been mentioned.

One way to force yourself to be a good listener, especially when your supervisor is talking, is to take notes. Think back to your school days. How much did you remember of classes in which you just sat and listened? Conversely, compare how much you learned from classes where you took good notes. No comparison.

You cannot be a good listener if you talk all the time or if you constantly seek an opening in order to get your two cents in while someone else is expounding. You can only be one if you keep your mouth shut and concentrate on what the other person is saying.

Getting noticed and being influential is not about talking. Vice President Dick Cheney was legendary for not saying anything in cabinet meetings, yet people certainly noticed him and no one doubted his enormous influence.

89. LEARN FROM OTHERS

Learning from others is directly related to good listening skills.

Every person you run across should be viewed as a fount of new knowledge. Chances are they come from very different backgrounds than you do, and that is to your advantage. Listening well and drawing people out about themselves and their experiences can be of great value. Since it is human nature to drone on and on about oneself, you should have no trouble eliciting information from the 99 percent of humanity who love to hear themselves talk.

What you want to discover during these interactions is what went right and what went wrong. Perhaps you can pick up a new way of doing something that always gave you trouble. Conversely, you can learn what not to do by the example of others. In either case, you will have absorbed useful life lessons.

90. PRACTICE TELEPHONE ETIQUETTE

Most people don't have to worry much about this anymore, and that is a shame. Thanks to the evils of voicemail and telephone loops, live bodies no longer answer most business phones. Callers are forced to listen to recorded messages that repeat how important their call is to the recipient. If it is that important, then a human being should be answering the phone.

My company never instituted such a system, our conviction being that clients deserved to speak to people with real blood flowing through their veins. For those of you who work in similarly enlightened legal organizations (fewer and fewer all the time), here are a few things to keep in mind:

- Telephone etiquette is related to remembering customer service, but is a bit broader than that. In the course of your job, you will probably have to deal with vendors, information sources, and a great many other people on the phone.
- Always treat everyone you speak to with respect. You never know who they might be or who they might become someday.
- It was not uncommon in our legal career transition consulting business for the two chief executives to answer the phone. Often when we did, the people at the other end of the line assumed we were the hired help and talked down to us. Big mistake.

These people were memorable. They became famous for the wrong reasons.

- Never use a client's or stranger's first name unless you are permitted or requested to do so. Otherwise, this kind of overfamiliarity is insulting and off-putting.
- When taking a message for someone in your office, note the date and time of the call, write down the name of the caller accurately (asking for the spelling if necessary), and repeat the phone number to the caller so that you note it correctly.
- Return calls promptly . . . and never more than 24 hours later.

91. ESCHEW HUBRIS

This is a "la-de-da" way of saying don't let your pride overcome your common sense.

One of my attorney clients called me one day very upset because her boss and two corporate bigwigs discussed her work product behind her back. She had prepared a corporate filing for the Securities and Exchange Commission and it went up the corporation's ladder for approval. When she discovered that her written work was the subject of discussion without her being present, she went ballistic, going so far as to demand that one of the senior officers of the company march right down to her office, where she bawled him out for having the audacity to do this to her.

I told her she was overreacting, permitting her ego to overwhelm her common sense. (She outlived her welcome in this company rather quickly and was soon let go.)

When you write something for an organization, you are writing what, in U.S. Copyright Office parlance, is called a "work for hire." In other words, you don't own it or have any proprietary rights to it. It belongs to the organization. Consequently, there is no place in a corporation or any other organization for what, in the civilian world, is called "pride of authorship." Your superiors have every right to discuss your work product whenever and wherever they so desire, with or without you present.

92. DEMONSTRATE ENERGY AND ENTHUSIASM

A can-do attitude is infectious and leaves good feelings all around. Moreover, attitude is almost as important as performance when the bosses get together to evaluate employees and make promotion and downsizing decisions.

Maintaining a positive attitude will also help you both emotionally and in terms of getting work done competently. People who grump around the office and exude negative vibes are highly inefficient, produce poor work product, feel bad about themselves, and are generally avoided by everyone else.

One of my early bosses had a wonderful mantra that he kept repeating: "Turn every job into a problem to be solved, and tackle the solution with enthusiasm."

The chief clerk of the U.S. Supreme Court once told me about hiring for a key position in his office. He asked every candidate how he or she felt about staying at work until midnight or later while the Court was finishing up its work for the year, having to get through all of the cases it had to consider before adjourning for the summer. With one exception, every candidate hesitated before half-heartedly responding, "Sure, I guess I could do that" or words to that effect. The woman who was hired for the job jumped right at the question and said, "I'm always eager to do whatever it takes to get the job done right."

A high energy level (or the appearance of one) leaves a tremendously favorable impression on those around you. You will find that displaying high energy contrasts markedly with most everyone else in the workplace (or elsewhere, for that matter). It will make you an irresistible magnet.

93. REMEMBER THE MANNERS YOUR MOTHER TAUGHT YOU

You cannot go wrong if you apply the common courtesies to the workplace. That means saying hello, please, thank you, and you're welcome (instead of the monumentally annoying "no problem"). Also, say "bless you" or some equivalent if someone sneezes.

The converse of this is equally important. Don't use bad language. The only four-letter word appropriate to the workplace is W-O-R-K. I am personally offended when people with whom I work curse or use foul language. Increasingly, some women think this is an important means of demonstrating their equality. They are wrong. It is a very effective way to demonstrate that you are an uncouth, boorish lout.

If someone in (or out of) your organization does something nice for you, send a thank-you note. If your boss does something nice for you, say thank you immediately. It is amazing how many people get a raise and never acknowledge it with an appreciative word to the boss. This happened to me countless times.

94. VOLUNTEER

If your job does not keep you busy, look for work outside of your regular work. The successful law firm attorneys I know comb their offices and go outside their practice groups to find work if they are short of it and may not be able to meet billable hour expectations.

There are few organizations where there is not enough to do to keep everyone busy. If you happen to end up in one of them, it probably means they do not have enough business. Offer to help them get more.

Make sure if you volunteer to help others in your spare time that your bosses know about it. There are many ways to alert them to your efforts without being overbearing about it.

95. BECOME THE GO-TO PERSON

Study the cutting-edge issues and cases of first impression that your trends analysis tells you are likely to crop up in your office, learning as much about them as you can before they emerge in your organization. Then, when they materialize, offer to tackle them.

Do this a few times and you will develop a reputation for being the person in the organization who others can turn to for advice and assistance with new matters.

There are ways to do this indirectly, too. An attorney at the U.S. Nuclear Regulatory Commission (NRC) who was proficient in Russian, thanks to his military intelligence stint years before, worked there for 15 years without having any occasion to employ his language skills. When the Chernobyl nuclear reactor meltdown occurred, he made it known around the agency general counsel office and beyond that he had Russian language skills and would be happy to assist any NRC office with questions arising from the Chernobyl disaster.

Within weeks, the NRC was barraged with questions from its Russian and Ukrainian counterparts about nuclear reactor safety and health effects, and this attorney was brought in to translate documents and serve as an interpreter whenever Soviet scientists and officials visited. Soon thereafter, the NRC decided that it needed a special office to deal with these matters, and this attorney was appointed to head it.

96. MAKE EVERYONE FEEL IMPORTANT

Other than money, everyone craves respect and occasional deferential treatment, at least enough to permit them to say to themselves once in a while, "I am somebody." Letting people know you respect them and treating them kindly and in a friendly manner pays big dividends. After all, you never know whom you might be giving the back of your hand and where and when your paths might cross in the future.

There is a great story—alas a widely circulated urban legend—that makes this point very well: A gentleman walked into the office of the president of Harvard University and asked if he could talk to the president for a few minutes. He told the secretary that he had something very important to say to him. The secretary was quite put out that someone would have the temerity to walk into the Harvard president's office without an appointment and be so brash as to request one on the spot. However, the gentleman was quite persistent, and finally the secretary relayed his request to the president. Unfortunately for Harvard, the president, who was not at all busy that day, said, "Tell him to make an appointment like everyone else if he wants to see me."

The young man, angry at being put off, hopped on a westbound train and did not get off until San Francisco. Instead of donating his millions to endow a building at Harvard, Leland Stanford established his own rival university in California.

97. HELP PEOPLE WITH THEIR PROBLEMS

The impression that you are a caring, responsible, and sensible individual will make its way around your office soon enough without much help from you.

Empathy is a powerful force in the workplace. Demonstrating sensitivity is critical to career success. We are all different, and when we come to work, these differences tend to become exaggerated by the economic and hierarchical pressures associated with working, plus whatever might be going on at home.

Most people come to the office with a lot of baggage: all of the grim things that happened to them before they worked there, as well as all the very recent large and petty annoyances of their domestic lives.

Nothing demonstrates this better than the surge in workplace violence, which has seeped beyond the U.S. Postal Service into the rest of the working world. Even law offices are not exempt. In the recent past, a large law firm in San Francisco was tragically victimized by a shooter on a rampage.

Be cognizant that virtually all of your colleagues come into the workplace every day boiling over with this stuff. If they bitch and moan about it, don't just shut them off. Show them that you understand and have some compassion.

Be available if one of your colleagues comes to you for advice. Just be careful not to overextend yourself at the expense of either your employer or common sense. If you are a lawyer admitted in California and someone in your office in Maine comes to you for free legal advice on a domestic matter, know your legal and ethical limitations. Remember, in Maine you are just an average person who went to law school. You are not a member of the Maine bar.

Remember, too, that every time you take time from your job to help a colleague with a personal problem, you are shortchanging the person who signs your paycheck. Suggest to the person seeking your assistance that you meet over lunch or after work to discuss his or her issues.

Also, don't muscle your way into people's lives in order to implement this advice. When I was a new boy scout, recently imbued with the "do a good deed every day" creed, I forcibly dragged an older lady across a busy street and only realized later that she did not want to cross the street at all, but was waiting for a taxi!

98. IMPROVE THE BUSINESS

A boss once advised me to tone down my efforts to improve the bottom line because that would put more pressure on our unit to do even better next year. I was shocked by her statement and immediately lost all respect for her. Less than six months later, she was replaced as the boss because the unit was not living up to expectations.

Part of your unwritten job description in any position is to improve the business and the bottom line. Every task you perform at work should be geared toward those goals. Lawyers, because of their unique support positions in organizations, are often surprised when I say this to them. One of the best questions that I recommend attorneys ask of corporate job interviewers is "How does the legal office contribute to shareholder value?" The question invariably throws off the attorney interviewer.

In addition to factoring the improvement question into your daily work, take some quality time to think creatively about other ways to improve the business. Remember that improving the business improves your own career opportunities.

99. FIND A NEW CUSTOMER

This is the essence of almost every private sector organization. If you are able to bring in a new customer, you will be remembered fondly when it counts.

People who work for large organizations tend, incorrectly, to think in "pigeonhole" terms: "I don't work in marketing or sales, so it is not up to me to bring in business."

Quite the contrary! It is up to you if you want the outfit that generates your paycheck to continue to be able to do so and if you want to make a name for yourself in the organization.

One simple way to get started on the right road toward this goal is to have business cards with you at all times and to remember to give them out to virtually everyone you meet. One of the best attorneys at client development that I ever encountered went to three different Denver churches every Sunday so that he could pass out his business cards to as many people as possible. While I hesitate to recommend such an over-the-top approach, there are many other arenas where you normally go that would lend themselves to a reasonable business development effort.

Attorneys are also much in demand for presentations to both attorney and non-attorney groups and organizations. A tax controversy practitioner client of mine sought every opportunity to make presentations about representing taxpayers before the Internal Revenue Service and the state tax authorities to local and regional associations of accountants and financial advisors. They, in turn, referred cases to his firm, for which he received credit.

A young lawyer who worked in the Washington, D.C., office of a major out-of-town law firm as a lobbyist for the trucking industry on environmental issues saw an opportunity in the fall of the Soviet Union. He approached the new Russian commercial attaché in Washington with the idea of establishing a U.S.-Russian trade council, to be launched with a presentation by a senior Russian government official. Several days later, the attaché called him and asked if the new Russian foreign minister would be a suitable presenter! The attorney immediately drafted an email to all of the Fortune 500 representatives in Washington, inviting them to the speech. Three hundred–plus corporate reps showed up and the attorney's law firm became the sole legal counsel to the new council. Note that his creative client development initiative had nothing whatsoever to do with trucks or the environment.

100. SELL SOMETHING ELSE TO AN EXISTING CLIENT/CUSTOMER

Persuading a new customer to take the plunge and buy what your law firm or company is selling is far more difficult than selling additional items to an existing customer who already knows about your organization and is (presumably) satisfied with what he or she purchased so far. Moreover, the initial prospecting to identify the customer has already been done, so no additional resources need be spent on overcoming that huge hurdle. The biggest advantage is that you will be dealing with a known quantity, not a mystery individual or firm.

Everyone who works in any capacity for any organization is, of necessity, immersed in marketing and sales all the time. Use that to your advantage.

101. LOOK FOR WAYS TO SAVE MONEY

What employer would let go of an employee who saves him or her money?

During my brief tenure as an employee, I once made a suggestion that was accepted and implemented and ended up saving my organization a substantial amount of money. Shortly thereafter, there was a downsizing in my organization that affected my tiny branch. Someone had to go. Although I had less seniority than others, I stayed on. Not because my boss liked me any better than the others. In fact, he probably liked me much less since I was, to say the least, an irritant, always questioning his judgment (usually a bad idea). However, what saved me was that no one else was making him look as good.

Analyze what you personally do every day and I am certain you will be able to devise more efficient ways of getting the job done. Money-saving ideas are all around you. You only have to keep your eyes open. Does your legal office, for example, store a lot of documents on site? Consider recommending off-site storage, such as is provided by companies like Iron Mountain, which will pick up and deliver records rapidly when requested. The space savings of off-site document storage can amount to a great deal of money. Does your unit have several printers when it could network into one shared printer? Does the office continue to contract for nightly trash pickup while simultaneously going paperless?

102. REMEMBER CLIENT/CUSTOMER SERVICE

You cannot go wrong being solicitous of clients and customers and dropping everything to help them resolve a problem. The problem does not necessarily have to be one that is related to your professional relationship with the client. It can be about anything. Just remember not to promise more than you might be able to deliver. And do not, in your eagerness to help, go beyond your capabilities.

Customer service is so bad throughout most of society that good customer service is almost as memorable an experience as one's first kiss.

103. RISE ABOVE THE CROWD

It should not take you long to observe the work habits of your coworkers and to note those that are pluses and the many more that are likely to be minuses. Once you have gathered that intelligence, sort through it for the items you can incorporate into your indispensability plan. In addition, systematically add the pieces of advice in this book to your plan. Finally, try if you can to determine the reasons why certain of your colleagues did not work out as employees and why others got promoted ahead of their coworkers.

You do not have to wait until you have all of this material in its entirety to begin implementing the positive pieces.

104. BECOME AN EXPERT

Find something no one understands or shies away from because of its complexity (e.g., knowledge management, website promotional pieces, legal blogs, carbon cap and trade, Daubert jurisprudence, the D'Oench Duhme doctrine, etc.), and learn it well enough to be considered the resident expert. Once you become widely known as *the* information resource in the organization, let it be known that you are available to anyone in the office and any client who needs your counsel.

You will find that your colleagues and, more importantly, your supervisors and managers will flock to you for advice and assistance. Soon, when they need help in the area you have staked out as your own, they will automatically think of you. That kind of credibility and reliability buys an awful lot of job security in today's hyper-volatile legal market.

In addition to developing a valuable niche for yourself, you will be setting yourself apart from the competition.

So how do you become an expert? Here is a surefire, three-step approach to establishing your expertise and consequent indispensability:

1. *Decide whom you want to reach.* You have to be able to identify the market for your expertise before you can decide about its scope (should it be narrow or broad?) and the vehicles you will choose in order to broadcast it to the market. You should be mindful that the market is, initially, your office colleagues.

2. *Ponder your prowess.* We are all experts at something, but often our particular specialty is so ingrained or subliminal that we are not even aware of it. Examine your credentials with care in order to align your particular strengths and interests with the needs of your organization and its members. Credentials are not necessarily equal to a sheepskin conferred upon you by an academic institution. They also include experience and even avocational activity, such as a hobby or a field of interest. As part of this self-analysis, ask yourself these questions:

- What am I good at?
- What do I enjoy doing?
- What do I do better than other people?
- What do I like to talk and/or write about?

3. *Promote yourself.* You can do this by:

- Talking to colleagues about your developing expertise
- Teaching a continuing legal education or other class or training session within the organization, as well as to outside groups
- Publishing something about your expertise (book, article, op-ed piece, etc.)
- Speaking to groups, professional or otherwise

It is truly amazing how instantly credibility can be achieved by taking these simple steps. The words "author of...," for example, can carry enormous weight with readers and others who hear of your activities.

105. BECOME AN IN-HOUSE CONSULTANT

If you become an expert in something, offer your consulting services to others in your organization. If you work for a company, government agency, or other legal department, go beyond just your office and offer your expertise, if relevant, to the entire organization. If you are in a law firm, go through the proper procedures to offer your consulting advice to firm clients.

When people take you up on your offer, your reputation for specialized knowledge will soon spread company-wide.

One extremely important additional point about law firms: they have gone into a dizzying array of ancillary (subsidiary) businesses in recent years, compelled by intense competition from other professional service firms for the legal and law-related dollar. Hundreds of law firms have established subsidiary businesses in order to (1) serve law-related and nonlegal needs of existing clients and (2) attract new clients who then will also request legal services.

Some of the more popular such businesses are as follows:

- Litigation consulting
- Litigation support/ document management
- Alternative dispute resolution services
- Insurance planning and recovery
- Insurance claims analysis and valuation
- Risk management services
- Training programs for clients and others, both on-site and online
- Loss advisory services
- Class action suit claims administration
- Employee relations and HR consulting
- Diversity recruiting, retention, and training
- Finance and trade consulting
- Venture capital brokering services
- Financial planning and advisory services
- Trust management
- Government relations and lobbying
- Public affairs consulting
- Crisis communications
- Campaign finance consulting
- Health-care consulting
- Web-based practice management for physicians
- Internet purchasing systems for medical organizations
- Medical records consulting
- E-commerce and biotechnology consulting
- Intellectual property asset management for corporations and universities
- Science-based consulting services to businesses and their legal counsel
- World Trade Organization consulting
- European Union trademark registration services

- Foreign shipping company compliance
- International finance and development
- International trade advisory services
- Political risk and market analysis
- Law office management technology
- Damage assessment, measurement, case strategy, and related research and analysis in connection with securities fraud and other complex litigation
- Forensic/investigative accounting services
- Registration agent services
- Crisis management and restructuring services for financially troubled businesses
- Environmental risk assessment
- Land acquisition and conservation
- Condemnation and appraisals
- Technology risk analysis
- Financial analysis for complex business transactions
- Business relocation
- Business performance enhancement
- Corporate development
- Capital market relations
- Project development
- Tax services
- IRS refund claims management
- Economic development consulting
- Governmental permitting
- Privatization
- Jury consulting services
- Electronic compliance
- Investment consulting for municipalities

These ancillary businesses vastly expand your opportunities to become an in-house consultant on issues of importance to your firm and its clients. Moreover, if you work for a law firm that has not yet delved into the provision of subsidiary professional services, this might be a wonderful opportunity that you can propose to the firm managers.

106. OFFER YOUR SERVICES AS A TRAINER

Training is BIG in America and in the global economy. Law firms, corporations, and public sector organizations pay a lot of money for outside consultants to come in and train their employees in a wide variety of hot-topic areas, from ethics to dispute resolution to sexual harassment sensitivity training.

By presenting yourself as a trainer in an area in which you have real expertise, you will be earning organizational capital for yourself while saving your employer money.

Involving yourself in your organization's internal training program also adds another facet to your "career personality," a valuable thing to have in good or bad times.

Developing a training base within your organization could also lead to a prominent role in selling the same or related training to outside organizations, clients, and customers. As you can see from the list of law firm ancillary businesses, a number of law firms have developed on-site and online training products that they market to existing and new clients. This then becomes a great way to lock in your value to your organization.

107. KEEP UP WITH TECHNOLOGY

Remember the guy in the television ad who recommends switching long distance companies to his boss, thereby impressing him with his perspicacity? Become that guy. He took the trouble to learn as much as he could about a technological option that could save his company money. You simply cannot go wrong earning a reputation as someone who looks for ways to save money by recommending technological improvements, all of which will also likely contribute to increased productivity.

There is a danger here. You can see it in kids all the time. It is the "Gameboy Syndrome," where they become so obsessed with the technology that every other facet of their lives becomes secondary. They spend whole days glued to the television or computer or hand-held video game watching technology do its magic, interacting with it, but to what end?

The mentality that turns these kids into pale and often obese couch potatoes with no other interests or activities in their lives is not peculiar to children. Adults can fall into the technology trap, too. There are many people who float around in cyberspace and have literally forgotten that there is also a parallel real world out there beyond Second Life. When they bought their computers and hooked up to the Internet, they sold their souls.

Technology is interesting and fun, so long as you know when to quit. However, for some people, it quickly becomes an addiction, and one that carries with it the seeds of possible ruination.

Never forget that a computer, a database, and Internet connectivity are merely tools to make us more efficient, not substitutes for living. If you fall into the virtual world and cannot (or don't want to) find your way out, you risk becoming roadkill on the Information Superhighway.

However, there is much to be gained from riding the technology wave. First, it is going to be increasingly important in the future to be conversant with new technologies, at least insofar as knowing how to milk them for your benefit. Second, most people run away from technology, so if you embrace it (at least platonically), you will gain a tactical advantage. Third, regard it as a useful tool to make you and your job more efficient.

108. PARTICIPATE IN THE INCENTIVE AWARDS PROGRAM

An increasing number of organizations—private and public—have incentive awards programs, where the person who suggests an improvement that winds up saving the organization money shares in the savings and is honored in other ways, too. This is an excellent way to underline how essential you are to the organization.

Moreover, in your quest to be an indispensable employee, you are already looking for places where processes and/or systems can be improved. They are not hard to find in any organization. And in outfits that have such an awards program, your reward can be both short term (cash bonuses) and long term (indispensability).

109. PROPOSE AT LEAST ONE SOLID IDEA A MONTH

With all that goes on in any organization, a flood of ideas is relatively easy to come by. If you keep a notebook with you at all times, you will always be able to write down interesting ideas as they occur to you. Some people (like me) even keep their notebooks at bedside in case they wake up in the middle of the night with a brilliant idea.

Over the many years that I have employed this technique, I have averaged over 15 ideas per month. Many of them fail to emerge into anything more than words jotted on paper, but a few survive further analysis and make it into the discussion.

However, think your idea through before going off half-cocked and announcing it to the world. Evaluate it from every angle. One rule I employ: Write it down in the heat of the exciting moment, then let it fester for at least a week. Then come back to it and see if you are still as excited about it. Often, once I calm down, I am much less thrilled by what I initially thought was my groundbreaking idea.

If you do this and you still feel excited about it, your idea might have promise. That is when you should invest some of your spare time into thinking it through and running it through your own devil's advocate test. If it passes, then maybe it's time to write it out in more detail and run with it.

Suggesting at least one well-conceived idea each month is a great way to keep your indispensability in front of the decision makers in your organization and will also provide you with strong material at annual review time. If any of your ideas make it through the analysis and implementation stages, you will have entrenched yourself solidly in your organization and your employer's good graces. And, since we live in a what-have-you-done-for-me-lately world, the one idea per month strategy will keep your creativity and constant striving to improve the organization in front of your managers.

110. FIND OPPORTUNITIES TO APPLY YOUR IDEAS

Naturally, if you are the type of person who generates a lot of ideas, you will be very eager to see some of them actually implemented. In order to make this happen, you will have to be diplomatic and also have your fingers constantly on the pulse of your organization. Even if testing out an idea means doing it in a modest, unspectacular way, do it when you can without doing harm to yourself.

I worked for a legal aid clinic while in law school and was provisionally admitted to the New York State Bar so that I could represent clinic clients in court. I had to draft a divorce pleading for my very first courtroom client and noticed that the recommended pleading form was very lengthy and that the suggested language contained countless "whereases" and "wherefores," as well as other legalisms that did not, in my opinion, add very much substance to the document and played soft and loose with plain English.

I went back and studied the statutory requirements for obtaining a divorce in New York State and discovered that none of this verbiage was required. That gave me an idea: instead of a multipage document filled with arcane words and phrases, I thought it might be possible to craft a pleading that was written in plain English on only one page.

My strategy was to prepare two alternative pleadings: one, the lengthy traditional version; the other, my new streamlined version.

Before going to court, I showed both versions to the clinic advisor and explained my research and rationale. He agreed with my conclusion and, bolstered by his approval, I submitted the streamlined version—and a memorandum supporting its use (which I prepared at the suggestion of my advisor)—to the judge. He looked at it and said, "Hmm, counselor, this is highly irregular. It only takes up three-quarters of a page. I'll have to review it and defer a ruling on its acceptability until then. Proceed."

I presented my case and, the next day, was summoned to the court to hear the judge's response. He accepted my streamlined pleading and announced to the assembled attorneys waiting for their cases to be tried that, henceforth in his court, he expected to see only divorce pleadings that followed my model.

I was flying high for days. From that point on in my career, I employed that same methodology. Every time I came up with an idea for doing something a different way, I proceeded methodically after extensive study and preparation of supporting arguments, and most importantly, was respectful of the chain of command.

lll. SEEK EVALUATIONS

If your organization does not do formal, periodic employee evaluations, and you know you are performing very well, ask your boss for one after three or six months on the job. Then ask for periodic ones at set intervals.

However, if there is any doubt, and you think you might not be pulling your weight, perhaps you should refrain from asking for an evaluation until you've mended your ways. Then immediately set yourself to working harder and smarter so that you will never again have to be uncertain about your level of effort or the quality of your work.

If you work in an organization that does provide formal employee evaluations at set intervals, and you know that you have performed very well on a particular project, make sure that you document your accomplishment for yourself, including any recognition (verbal, written, or other) you received for your performance. Many of my legal career transition clients have lamented the fact that they were praised for something they did, but cannot remember exactly what it was or the content of the commendation. You will not have that problem if you draft a memorandum for your records at the time you receive the pat on the head for a job well done.

Building up a personal record of such commendations can be of immense value at review time if your review is less than outstanding. This can be very important in a law firm setting where reviews are often done by more than one attorney, some of whom may be too distant from your daily work to know how you have performed on specific projects. Usually—but not always—these reviewers tend to defer to your immediate supervisor and go along with his or her review. Also, being only human, reviewers do not always just stick to your performance merits (or demerits), but let their personal feelings about you intervene. Many firms permit you to draft a rebuttal to an adverse review. In those circumstances, your documentation of praise received can be vital to your future career at the firm.

112. STRIVE TO BE THE BEST AT EVERYTHING YOU DO

The advice in this book begins with doing whatever is necessary to master your own job. Once you have that under control, you can volunteer for the tough assignments and put your all into them. You can test yourself and learn as much as possible about the outer limits of your work and capabilities. You will be in a position to make yourself the one the boss comes to when he or she has a problem.

Putting yourself in a position to be that kind of indispensable asset to your employer goes beyond the workday. As we've already discussed, it means coming in ready to work, doing what is necessary to transform yourself into an expert in the job, and so much more.

However, being the best requires even more.

113. PROTECT YOUR POSITION

Most of the indispensability strategies in this book urge you to go on offense. That means taking positive, affirmative steps designed to solidify your position within the organization. At the same time, however, you need to be aware of the defensive measures necessary to protect your position in the organization.

Great performance on the job and stellar relations with your colleagues and managers are the keys to job survival, security, success, and satisfaction, but they are not always enough to assure your status. Defense is equally important, both in an organizational sense and as a tactic to insulate yourself against the envy and ill will that some people will inevitably manifest toward you.

A law student at the top of her class did all of the right things to make herself shine among her peers: she earned top grades, won a number of CALI awards (given in many law schools to the student achieving the highest grade in a class), made law review, wrote for a school newsletter, was president of the Women's Law Caucus, served as a recruiting advocate for her law school, etc.

During one final examination, she inadvertently violated a minor technical rule, of which she was completely unaware, with respect to starting the exam and was immediately turned in to the school's honor committee by a jealous fellow student. She received an email notification that, among other possible punishments, she could be expelled from law school.

She survived the investigation and continued to perform at the top of her class, but at great emotional cost. Her traumatic experience taught her that playing great offense was not enough; she also had to play great defense. In her case, great defense meant taking the time to educate herself on all of the tedious test-taking rules and school honor code admonitions that could have prevented her from having to endure such a difficult and stressful ordeal.

114. GET CREDENTIALED

This is an important career step that you can undertake in order to secure your position and promote yourself. Getting yourself certified is important, mainly because it influences so much else:

- *Certification gives you an official paper credential,* confirming that you have studied or been trained in a particular specialty. That can overcome a lot of questions and skepticism and provide something of an insurance policy at crunch time.
- *Certification is a credibility enhancer.* If you have a knack for website design and are eager to demonstrate that knack, a certificate that you went through a training program in Web development will enhance your perceived value to the organization over and above the practical application of your Web skills.
- *Being able to include a credential on your résumé can result in accelerated promotion or transfer within the organization* (important if your practice area dries up). Although possession of the formal credential may be essentially meaningless, without it you are out of luck if the job description or announcement demands it.
- *Credentialing sets you apart from the competition.* All other factors being equal, the person with a certificate looks more impressive and will likely get the promotion or transfer. Sometimes this happens even if all factors are not equal.

For example, two individuals I know both worked for the same government regulatory agency when an opportunity arose to head an exciting new division responsible for establishing and administering scientific exchange programs with China. Both applicants spoke Mandarin Chinese. One was perfectly fluent, having learned it at home because his parents were Chinese émigrés. The second one learned it at the highly respected Defense Language Institute in Monterey, California, but was not nearly as accomplished in Mandarin as the person who grew up speaking it every day at home. The native speaker just assumed that everyone knew he must be proficient in Mandarin, given his background. Nevertheless, the second applicant's résumé mentioned his Defense Language Institute certificate in a profile at the top of the document, and he got the job.

Some credentials are easier to obtain than others. A professional degree, for example, takes a lot of time, effort, and money. Studying for, taking, and passing a bar examination in order to practice law is a daunting experience. Clearly, those undertakings are not something one typically does in one's spare time (although it is surprising how many hardworking, ambitious, driven people are, in fact, able to pursue demanding education programs and licenses after hours and on weekends).

At the same time, there are certificates and professional designations that are relatively effortless to obtain. These can often be secured online or on weekends and evenings in brick-and-mortar settings. In addition, continuing professional education programs are rapidly becoming popular across an increasing number of fields, and many of these grant certificates at the end of the training.

There are a large number of these available in legal and law-related fields, including:

- Alternative Dispute Resolution
- Americans with Disabilities Act
- Anti-Money Laundering
- Art and Museum Law
- Banking and Finance Regulation
- Bankruptcy Law
- Biopharmaceutical Regulatory Affairs
- Biotechnology and Intellectual Property
- Business Ethics
- Child Welfare Law
- Civil Trial Advocacy
- Clean Air Compliance
- Clean Water Compliance
- Compliance (General, Health Care, Tax, Securities, Occupational Safety and Health, Investment Advisor, Credit Union, Insurance, Export, etc.)
- Copyright and Related Rights
- Corporate Governance
- Corporate Restructuring
- Creditors' Rights
- Criminal Justice
- Criminal Trial Advocacy
- Doing Business in China
- Drug Development
- E-Commerce
- E-Commerce and Intellectual Property
- Economic Development
- Elder Law
- Employee Benefits Law
- Employee Handbooks
- Employee Relations
- Employment Law
- Energy Finance
- Energy Risk Management
- Enforcement of Maritime Claims
- Environmental Ethics
- Environmental Law
- Environmental Policy
- Environmental Regulation
- Estate Planning Law
- Ethics
- EU Maritime and Shipping Law
- Executive Compensation
- Family Law
- Family Mediation
- Financial Crimes
- Fraud Examination

- General Agreement on Trade in Services
- Global Arbitration Law and Practice
- Government Contracts and Procurement
- Guardianship
- Hazardous Waste Compliance
- Health Care Ethics
- Health Care Risk Management
- Health Law
- Health Policy
- HIPAA Privacy Rules and Portability
- Historic Preservation
- Homeland Security
- Information Privacy
- Intellectual Asset Management
- Intellectual Property
- International Business
- International Dispute Settlement
- International Food Law
- International Law and Practice
- International Law of the Sea
- International Marine Environmental Law
- International Tax Law
- International Trade Documentation
- International Trade Finance
- International Trade Law
- Investment Banking
- Labor Relations
- Land Use and Environmental Planning
- Law of International Institutions
- Law Office Management
- Law of Marine Collisions
- Law of Marine Insurance
- Law of Maritime Safety
- Legislative Studies
- Licensing
- Legal Investigation
- Legal Nurse Consulting
- Legal Professional Liability
- Maritime Labor Law
- Maritime Legislative Drafting
- Marketing for Lawyers
- Medical Devices Regulatory Affairs
- Medical/Legal Consulting
- Medical Professional Liability
- Natural Resources Law and Policy
- Negotiation

- Nonprofit Management
- Patient Advocacy
- Pharmacy Law
- Planned Giving
- Real Estate
- Risk Management
- School Risk Management
- Shipping Law
- Social Security Disability

- Sports Agent Representation
- Sports Law
- Taxation
- Technology Transfer
- Training
- Victim Advocacy
- Water Conflict Management

115. LEARN HOW TO DO MORE THAN ONE THING

You have probably heard about the concept of cross-training. In the sports context, cross-training means using more than one training method in order to achieve your athletic goal—swimming and rowing, for example. In the workplace, cross-training means learning more than just one skill.

Everyone in today's work environment should have at least one fallback position. That means knowing how to do something else besides your job that could benefit your organization . . . or save your job. If you develop a "pigeonhole mentality" about your job, you may end up being the pigeon.

It bears repeating that the best thing you can learn how to do (if it is not already part of your job description) is market and sell your organization's product. In the final analysis, that is what every organization is all about.

116. MASTER A RELATED JOB

This is likely to be the easiest transition for you. If you are a good legal writer, seek opportunities to expand your legal writing capabilities to areas other than the ones you do all the time. Request the opportunity to expand your legal writing horizons by writing for business development purposes, for example. Newsletters, alerts, blogs, white papers—these are all devices that law firms now employ to keep in touch with clients and to attract new clients. Some firms even offer products for which they charge a fee, such as treatises on specific areas of law or developments in the law.

Keeping clients apprised about what is going on in areas of interest to them is not limited to law firms. There are many such opportunities available in every legal realm, be it an in-house counsel office in a corporation, a government legal office, a nonprofit whose constituents and donors need to be up-to-date, etc.

I emphasize writing because (1) a large portion of any attorney's job consists of written work product, (2) attorneys need to be able to explain complex issues in writing in order to succeed, (3) any outside writing that you do will improve the technical drafting skills you employ daily on the job, and (4) if you add client development and retention writing to your skill set, you are getting a double benefit that will make you even more essential to your employer.

However, you do not need to limit yourself only to writing when it comes to mastering a related job. Attorneys are also, presumably, good oral advocates, whether in a courtroom, in an administrative forum, at a negotiating table, or when counseling a client. Look for other opportunities to add to your oral presentation résumé, such as teaching a continuing legal education course, providing training to other attorneys and/or support staff in your office, making presentations to local groups, etc. Again, any of these sidelines will improve your oral advocacy skills while simultaneously attracting the attention of your organization's decision makers in a positive way.

You can also make an effort to become knowledgcable about related practice areas. If you happen to be a real estate transactional attorney, a good insurance policy might be to learn as much as you can about real estate distress law and/or bankruptcy law for when the real estate market turns down, as it inevitably will. In so doing, you are adding value to both yourself and your organization.

Most of you will not have to think too hard about areas related to your own education or work. Every job has several areas closely related to it. Ideally, you will take the time to become adept at all of them.

117. LET THE WORLD KNOW

This suggestion is closely related to the recommendation immediately above. Throw aside your inhibitions and make sure that you are your own best self-promoter. If you put in the sweat equity to expand your capabilities, do not keep it to yourself.

However, you need to be careful about how you undertake self-promotion. Modest, understated mentions of your newly acquired expertise are likely to be more effective than the overt, in-your-face, braggadocio approach.

118. TAKE ADVANTAGE OF TRAINING AND EDUCATIONAL OPPORTUNITIES

Many employers offer training and education programs to employees. Some of these are mandatory, but many more are optional. It is surprising how many people ignore these opportunities to improve their knowledge and skills—and thus become more indispensable employees.

You should take advantage of as many training opportunities as you can in areas related to your career. Do this even if it is not offered by your employer and you have to pay for it out of your own pocket. It will be more than worth the expense.

Who knows, you may actually learn something of value. And training always looks good on a résumé.

Of course, let your colleagues and bosses know that you have acquired additional training.

119. WRITE YOUR OWN JOB DESCRIPTION

No one enjoys writing job descriptions. That includes the human resources (HR) office personnel specialists who are trained to write them. It is a dull, boring, thankless task that promises considerably more pain than pleasure. As a result, it is often easy to get permission to write your own job description. In HR's eyes, you are doing them a favor.

Getting to write the official job description for your own job is a golden opportunity. You can use it to your great advantage. Official job descriptions are often reviewed by senior HR and other company officers—as well as outside workforce consultants specifically brought in for this purpose—when key decisions are about to be made about promotions, terminations, or restructuring. The information in job descriptions often determines who gets transferred to Toad Suck Ferry, Arkansas, and who gets to stay in the Big Apple. In other words, it can decide who is expendable . . . and who is indispensable. You want to have as much say in this decision-making process as possible. The best way to do that is to take advantage of any opportunity to write your own job description.

Job descriptions generally get written, rewritten, or updated under the following conditions:

1. *When there is no written job description.* This is a good opportunity to recommend that written descriptions might be needed and to volunteer to prepare your own. After all, you can suggest, no one knows your job better than you do.

2. *When the job has changed and a new, updated job description is needed.* Once you establish a pattern of revising your job description periodically when prompted by a change in your responsibilities, you will have established a valuable precedent for yourself. Of course, you would not want to revise the description if the change in your duties diminished or had other negative ramifications. In that case, it is best to leave the job description as is and hope that no one else decides it needs to be revised "downward."

3. *When no one has bothered to look at the job description in years.* Find out if this is the case, and then volunteer to update your description and to keep it current.

4. *When an outside consulting firm has been hired to come in and examine the job breakdown in the organization, generally with an eye to cutting costs (translation: layoffs).* This is the worst possible scenario for suggesting that your job description be revised, because this is truly the 11th hour. Nevertheless, you should still make the effort. If you get wind that this is imminent, do not hesitate. Use any legitimate and plausible rationale for getting at your job description, e.g.: it is no longer accurate because my responsibilities have changed; it does not reflect my performance bonus from last year; it has not been updated in a long time; etc.

When you develop the new job description, make sure you personalize it to accentuate your positives and downplay your negatives. *As much as possible, write it so that you are the only person on the planet who could possibly fill the position.* This is your chance to lock yourself in and make yourself indispensable.

You should regard this assignment as an opportunity for some very creative thinking. As long as you understand the importance of such a document, you can tailor it to your best advantage.

Sometimes, your employer might give you a form to complete that, once you have entered all the information, will serve as your job description. It is rare these days that the assignment is totally open-ended, without any guidelines provided by your employer (or worse, by the "efficiency experts" hired by your employer).

The types of questions on position description forms almost always fall into two categories: "home run" questions and "dangerous ground" questions.

Home run opportunities are those questions that invite you to shine, to "dazzle the reader with footwork," to hit them out of the ballpark. How do you recognize them?

The answer is simple: any question or category that offers you an opportunity to present yourself in the best possible light and/or to distinguish yourself from others in a positive way is a home run question.

Typical home run questions are the following:

- How would you describe the main purpose of your position?
- How does your position contribute to the organizational mission?
- What are the long-term goals of this position?
- What are the major (quantitative and/or qualitative) results or performance levels that can be expected from this position over the next several years?
- What are the responsibilities of this position?
- What are the key skills required for this job?

Here are a few suggestions for how to use your response to this type of question to solidify your position in the organization:

- If you work for a publicly traded corporation with shareholders, the purpose of every position is *to maximize shareholder value.* Period. Of course you will want to lead with this nice, safe, mainstream statement, then follow with a few things that are in your power to do in order to achieve this worthy goal. Those items are your contribution to the mission.

- Long-term goals should be exemplary ones, like reducing the cost of annual meetings by 10 percent, and they should also be achievable. Do not make the classic mistake of throwing out some lofty goals that someone in the organizational hierarchy can throw back at you a few years later and use as weapons against you. Pick goals that are good for the organization and *that you know you can meet,* yet ones that sound good to the reader.

- Responsibilities and skills necessary to your position are the ones you can really hit out of the park. Make sure your responsibilities are massive, central to the survival and functioning of the organization, and tremendously impressive. The skills necessary to do the job should be the ones you possess and should, if possible, be ones that are difficult to find in the marketplace.

Dangerous ground–type questions, in contrast, are those sections of a position description where you could destroy yourself if you are not careful. For example:

- How can your effectiveness be measured?
- What are the main objectives of your position?

- Describe the problems and difficulties associated with this position.

Here are a few suggestions for responding to this type of question in ways that are designed to bolster your position in the organization:

If you are asked how your effectiveness can be measured, give the evaluator some measurement standards that you are rock-solid certain to meet. Similarly, the main objectives of your position should be ones that are (1) closely related to the core mission of the organization and (2) achievable without straining the questioner's credulity. If you are asked about the problems and difficulties associated with your position, pick out only a handful and make sure that they do not come across as so insurmountable that you become suspected of not being able to surmount them!

120. WRITE THE PROCEDURES MANUAL FOR YOUR ACTIVITY

Every organization welcomes procedures manuals that will help them routinize the things they regularly do: for example, training new employees, or making the entity more efficient. Very few people like to write them, however. Like job descriptions, these are not exactly exciting, inspiring, or dramatic documents. If you offer to write one, you underline the fact that you are the expert in a particular area, and you will be consulted by others in the organization when they need relevant advice about the manual topic.

This kind of assignment also gives you an opportunity to devise a manual that reflects your way of going about your business, which can only make you look good when crunch time comes and some higher-up is weighing your performance against the written gospel.

One word of warning: There is a downside to this. My wife once wrote a detailed manual governing all the procedures necessary to run a college bookstore. It was so good and so easy to follow that when her boss's job was jeopardized, he used her manual to argue that the college could safely let my wife go instead of him, since he could now easily do both jobs.

The lesson from this is that if you are writing a procedures manual, don't put everything in it and don't make it appear that anyone following the manual's checklists can easily do the job.

121. INVOLVE YOURSELF IN LONG-TERM PROJECTS

One of my company's outplacement client firms announced that it was eliminating 450 positions (including 135 legal positions) in a company-wide downsizing. I asked the coordinator of the restructuring operation how the corporation had made the decision whom to cut and whom to keep.

She told me that, among other factors, they looked at the projects people were assigned and, in more cases than not, opted to retain the ones who were engaged in long-term projects that were in the middle of being performed. The company perceived these people to be more vital to its future than similarly situated individuals whose assignments were short term, albeit important.

There is an obvious lesson here: the more long-term projects in which you can participate, the less likely it is that you will be singled out for job elimination.

122. KEEP CAREFUL RECORDS

You never know when you will be called upon to justify some activity you did months or years ago or when you might need to construct a work history in order to get a promotion. It is a lot easier to record what you have done when you do it than to have to reconstruct it at a later time.

Anything important—a conversation, a phone call, a meeting—merits a brief memorandum and storage in an important place.

123. KEEP DETAILED RECORDS OF YOUR ACCOMPLISHMENTS

My legal career transition clients invariably neglect to mention some of their proudest achievements as employees when I do an initial intake and question them about their careers. It usually takes some prodding from me to get them to reveal some of the most important career information about themselves:

"Did you ever get recognized for going above and beyond your job description?"

"Now that you mention it, I did get an achievement award and a cash bonus for settling the Endicott employment discrimination class action favorably for our client."

"How come I don't see that reflected on your résumé?"

"I guess I forgot about it until now."

Frequently, my questions unleash a flood of positive outcomes and legal triumphs completely missing from the client's résumé.

A typical practitioner handles numerous cases at any one time. Over time, memories fade and accomplishments are forgotten.

Keep an ongoing, continually updated file of your achievements. Document them in narrative form. The example below (redacted to preserve client privacy) is a superb example of what I suggest:

Establishing a National Environmental Program

Problem

As a result of the banking crisis of the late 1980s and early 1990s, I was called upon to establish and lead several major new programs during a time of rapidly changing law and business operations at the FDIC. During this period, the FDIC was confronted with record numbers of bank failures and large volumes of assets—the majority being real estate assets—from failed banks to sell. We needed to resolve failed banks with minimum disruption to the banking system and to millions of depositors (the public) while maximizing revenues from sales of assets from failed banks in order to repay the Bank Insurance Fund.

I was assigned the responsibility of supervising legal services nationwide in the area of environmental law. I was challenged to develop an environmental program and quickly provide essential legal services at the same time that the FDIC was absorbing staff transferred from a closed agency—the Federal Savings and Loan Insurance Corporation (FSLIC)—and establishing many new field offices nationwide.

Analysis

In examining the matter, it became readily apparent that environmental issues had to be factored into the disposition of tens of billions of dollars of real estate assets assumed by the FDIC from failed institutions, and that this had to be accomplished as soon as possible. If not, the FDIC risked the likelihood of having to defend hundreds of lawsuits as well as potential liability for environmental cleanups costing billions of dollars.

Proposed Solution

Consequently, I mapped out a far-reaching national program that included a proposed budget, an estimate of manpower requirements, a strategy for incorporating environmental considerations into real estate dispositions, a template for analyzing environmental risks associated with real estate assets, and a timeline for implementation of my proposal.

Implementation

My success in persuading the business operations client of the importance and urgency of environmental laws and issues—and in proposing a systematic agency-wide program to manage them—is reflected by the fact that the FDIC established environmental policies and procedures nationwide and by the fact that the FDIC hired environmental attorneys and program specialists in all of its 26 field offices.

Results

Moreover, the nationwide program that I designed proved so successful that the FDIC was *never successfully challenged regarding any environmental matters* it inherited when it took over hundreds of failed banks and thrifts during this time period.

I received an FDIC Meritorious Service Award—the highest honor the agency can confer—for this achievement, along with a substantial cash bonus.

124. ALWAYS CONSIDER THE WORST CASE

Before you act, set aside your enthusiasm for the obvious upsides of your proposed action and think hard about the potential pitfalls. Organizations, for the most part, are risk averse, that is, they are not about going out on a limb. On the contrary, they are generally quite conservative. This, despite an extensive cottage industry consisting of seminars and retreats and consultants, all of which are paid considerable sums by organizations to come in and give them pep talks about "daring to be great," "lunging for the brass ring," and "going out on a limb," among other exhortations. Curious, isn't it?

Don't be deluded by all of this psychobabble into thinking anyone really means it...or believes it. Make sure that you think through all of the ramifications of a suggestion before putting it forward.

125. CONDUCT PERIODIC CAREER AUDITS

From time to time, stop and assess where you are in your career, where you have been, and where you want to be in a year and in five years, ultimately. If you are not satisfied with the audit results, take the necessary steps to make a midcourse correction.

A career audit is a very valuable, almost essential, exercise. It gives you the opportunity to step back from the daily fray and take stock of your job situation, your career path, your ambitions, your goals. If done correctly, it can be a very interesting, even energizing, experience.

A career audit is simply a shorthand term for an assessment of where you are in your career in relation to where you started out and where you are going. It should, at a minimum, consist of an updating of your résumé; consideration of whether to tailor additional résumés to specific types of employers or positions in your current organization for which you might be suited; your formal position description (if you work for an organization that has such a thing); a refinement of your bio, i.e., what you would enclose in a contract proposal or give to an outfit before which you are scheduled to speak (do this even if you never engage in those sorts of activities); an evaluation of your education and any further educational or training needs necessary to advance your career, the state of your credentials, and any other improvements required for you to position yourself to survive and progress.

At a minimum, your career audit will provide you with one or more timely, serviceable résumés in the event you might need them. Beyond that, it can serve as a business plan for the near term.

126. LEARN TO REASON ASSOCIATIVELY

If I had to sum up what makes a person a successful employee, it would be this: he or she is highly adept at connecting the dots.

Connecting the dots—or associative reasoning—is probably the most important factor separating successful people from the rest of the population. At the same time, the ability to connect the dots is an extremely elusive one that makes it a rare commodity in the workplace or anywhere else.

The ability to connect the dots—to see the relationships between disparate bits of information—is a critically important thinking skill, never more so than now, when we live in an age of information overload that is only going to become more confusing as time goes on. Unfortunately, this is a skill that you must come by on your own. It is not generally taught anywhere in the educational cycle.

Perhaps the closest we come to wrapping our minds around this concept is in the analogies sections of the Scholastic Aptitude Test (SAT) and its offspring, the Law School Admissions Test (LSAT), the Graduate Record Examination (GRE), and the Graduate Management Admissions Test (GMAT), to name a few that attorneys might have encountered. Here is an example:

Home runs are to touchdown passes as:

A. Attendance is to ticket prices
B. Forearms are to bat speed
C. Steroids are to weight training
D. A and C, but not B
E. All of the above
F. None of the above

Anyone who has torn his or her hair out or gone into shock over these test analogies knows how difficult it is to come up with a correct answer.

To a great extent, this book is an attempt to teach you how to connect the dots, to see the interconnections between what, at first glance, appear to be distinct matters. If you learn how to do that, you will be miles ahead of your competition.

Look for the connections in everything you do and everything that happens around you. Trends analysis, which was addressed in chapter 2, is a good training mechanism for learning to reason this way. If you apply it to your short-, medium-, and long-term career goals as well as your organizational objectives, you will boost your opportunities for job security, satisfaction, and success many times over.

Chapter 4

Major Workplace "Don'ts"

*I*N CHAPTERS 1 THROUGH 3, you learned how to do all of the positive
things that start you off on the right foot in a new job, build your value
to the organization, and secure your livelihood and future.

Sometimes all the positive things you do to ensure your job security
are not enough. It is also important to avoid the negatives, the boners, the
screwups, and the glitches that can ruin in a heartbeat all the good work
you have done to nurture a great employment situation. The major ways
employees destroy their credibility and expend all of the capital on the credit
side of their balance sheets are the focus of this section.

The advice in chapter 4 derives from direct and sometimes daily feedback from legal employers with whom I have worked about the biggest
mistakes their attorneys have made and the reasons why they did not last
in their jobs. The chapter goes a step further and instructs attorneys on
how to avoid those often fatal errors.

127. DON'T PLAY DURING WORK HOURS

There is a reason why you are at work. It is to produce, and in return, to earn compensation. If you take time away from your responsibilities to schmooze, to gab on the phone with your friends, to play computer games, or to wander the hallways seeking conversation, you are not producing. And your employer will notice.

128. DON'T LET YOUR BIORHYTHMS
GET IN THE WAY OF WORK

If you feel bad, suck it up. Don't announce your malaise to the whole office. Everyone has bad days, and you will probably garner less sympathy than you think you deserve. Try to hide your discomfort. It's only a few hours out of your life. However, if you feel particularly miserable, consider whether you are likely to be contagious and need to stay at home rather than risk exposing everyone else.

129. DON'T BRING YOUR PERSONAL
PROBLEMS TO WORK

When you close the door to the office at the end of the workday, you are likely to be thinking of how you are going to enjoy your evening or weekend. Presumably, you are not taking the job home: neither tangibly, as evidenced by a briefcase (or memory stick) full of work, nor intangibly, as "emotional baggage." You just want to forget about the job until you have to think about it again the next morning or on Monday.

You owe your employer the same treatment. When you come to work, your total concentration should be on your responsibilities. Don't go around whining about your domestic problems, especially not to your boss. It is unprofessional. He or she does not need to hear it.

130. DON'T ALLOW YOURSELF TO
BE DISTRACTED

Work demands concentration. Interrupting to answer extracurricular emails, playing solitaire on your computer, surfing the Web, leaving work to do personal errands, etc. do not belong to the workday.

131. DON'T BECOME MIRED IN THE PAST

The past might be prologue, and the lessons of history are certainly worth studying and learning well, if only to avoid the mistakes people made back then, but you don't want to yearn for the vaunted days of yore too openly or avidly. They are over and neither you nor the company can go back to them. Pining for the past is irrelevant and unfair to your colleagues who have to concentrate on future survival.

My company was a very successful legal publication firm for many years, dominating its market niche. Suddenly, the Internet was upon us, and we had no choice but to transition from print to online publishing. It was an excruciating ordeal, akin to starting all over again. Suddenly we were faced with numerous competitors, daily rather than monthly deadlines, and the demands of an audience newly accustomed to instant gratification and the ability to go elsewhere for comparable information and services with merely a mouse click. The market perception was that we were no longer unique, but had become commoditized.

While we might all have achingly daydreamed about past successes and the unfairness of their sudden disappearance, few members of the organization said so out loud. The ones who did were both annoying and distracting to those of us desperately fighting to regain our niche.

The future is now and tomorrow. Rather than waste time dreaming about past glories, you will be better served to think long and hard about how you will deal with what the future will throw at you and your organization.

132. DON'T GET COMPLACENT

Satisfaction with your achievements, your past successes, is a very dangerous game. Ask any professional athlete. It is not enough to say, "But last year I won the Triple Crown and was voted Most Valuable Player," when this year your batting average is exceeded by your weight and you can't buy a hit.

"What have you done for me lately?" is a concept not unique to the sports world. It is just as prevalent in the business world. Only the present and the future count. If that were not the case, the 8 million employees let go to date (through September 2009) during the Great Recession, plus the 9.1 million working part-time because either their hours have been cut back or they cannot find a full-time job, would still be at their mostly high-wage jobs instead of scrambling to feed their families and pay the mortgage or rent.

133. DON'T PROCRASTINATE

One of the worst things you can do is let yourself become bogged down. Whether it's in paper, in letting decisions pile up, in letting important emails or telephone messages go, or whatever. Don't let it happen. You will regret it. You will lose respect. You will become totally disorganized. You will forget important things.

As I keep emphasizing, try to deal with things only once. Don't revisit them over and over again. I know a businessman who picks up the same piece of mail 10, 15, 20 times before doing something about it, either throwing it away or responding to it. His office looks like chaos theory made manifest. Sometimes important items get lost this way, much to everyone's chagrin.

Procrastination is bad enough when you are dealing with petty matters. It can be disastrous when contemplating difficult decisions. True, tough decisions take careful thought and should never be made precipitately and without considering all important aspects. Nevertheless, that said, one of the worst things you can do is dither around and delay until it is too late, and you find that all of your input and consideration has really gotten you nowhere, and you are still making the decision in haste.

If you are prone to this terrible habit, break it now.

134. DON'T SECOND-GUESS YOURSELF

Monday morning quarterbacking is an American trait of which we should not be particularly proud. "I told you so" does not sound good in any language, even English.

Make like a snake. Once you molt out of your old skin, let it go. Don't worry about it anymore. It is a waste of energy and time. You cannot do anything about it. So why try?

Have you noticed that most of the people you know shuffle through life full of regrets? "If only I had gone to college when I was 18 years old." "If only I had majored in accounting rather than Siberian dance." "If only I had taken that first job in Tahiti rather than the one in Moose Bottom, Manitoba." "Boy, would my life be different now!"

Maybe. Maybe not. But rather than running around full of regrets, take life by the throat and do something about it. It is never too late to correct a mistake. You have to try. Unless, of course, you really enjoy wallowing in all the second-guessing and self-pity that attend regrets.

Everyone makes mistakes. Not every decision is unerringly correct. But once you realize it, either make it right or do something else constructive to overcome its bad effects. Whichever choice you make, don't sit around stewing over it.

135. DON'T BE ABSENT

Technically, you get to take time off only after you have earned it. While many organizations permit employees to invoke vacation days and sick leave before they have earned them, that does not mean that they like doing it.

Bosses like employees who are always at work when they are supposed to be there. They tend to appreciate them more than those who are gone too much of the time. No employee ever knows what "too much" means in this context. It is better to assume that it means any absence that is not earned and warranted. This kind of behavior all gets weighed and assessed when crunch time comes around.

If you have to see a doctor and it is not an emergency, try to make the appointment before or after the workday or on Saturday if the doctor will see you then. Same with repairmen coming to your house.

136. DON'T KEEP YOUR WHEREABOUTS
A SECRET

One of the most annoying things you can do to your boss and coworkers is to vanish when they come looking for you. If you are not where you are expected to be, it will be remembered, especially when key decisions concerning your future are reached. This is particularly true if you make a habit of evaporating at critical times. And remember, anytime your boss wants to see you is a critical time.

Unless you work in an environment where lunch is at a scheduled time every day, make sure before you go to lunch that (1) you have adequately covered your responsibilities before taking off, and (2) an appropriate person (boss, office manager) knows that you are going out to lunch.

I once worked for a large law office whose deputy general counsel roamed the corridors keeping a chart of people's whereabouts. If you were absent when the deputy came around, your absence was duly noted and ultimately would have to be explained to her satisfaction.

Needless to say, this behavior tended to make employees rather fearful of leaving their desks for any reason. The more paranoid among them even strained as long as they could tolerate to deny calls of nature.

While this was one of the paramount reasons I left the job shortly after joining the organization, once I became an employer, I began to see that, within reason, it had its merits.

We had a rule in my company that the powers-that-be must be informed in advance of planned absences, regardless of the reason for the absence. If something occurred between evening and morning to cause a person to either come in late or not at all, notice had to be given by telephone as soon as possible.

Even if you work in an office without such a rule, you should operate as if that rule were in place. That is only good manners as well as good common sense.

137. DON'T GIVE YOUR SENSE OF HUMOR FREE REIN

In these politically correct times, almost any joke is offensive to someone. The trouble with the workplace is you never know whom you might offend. Ethnic jokes have, perhaps, the greatest potential for being offensive, followed closely by jokes with a sexual tone to them. It is probably best to save them for the locker room or the Saturday night poker club.

I once drew what I thought was a completely harmless, rather humorous cartoon as a contribution to the weekly departmental football pool tout sheet. Everyone got a good guffaw out of it—except one person utterly lacking in any sense of humor whatsoever. In fact, her reaction was so off-the-wall and so extreme that I got into trouble with the big bosses for my feeble attempt at humor.

138. DON'T FORGET WHOSE MONEY IT IS

Many times employees have come to me with suggestions for spending my money. Some of these were well thought out; most were not. In fact, most were full of a huge dose of ignorance and a smidgen of arrogance. What the majority of suggestions like this have in common is their cavalier attitude toward, if not outright contempt for, the bottom line.

Someone once asked me for a car phone and fax so that she would be able to continue working while commuting the 45 minutes it took her to go between home and office. Since she was not even coming close to pulling her weight during working hours, the request, needless to say, was denied. She also went immediately on my watch list.

Another person told me she could do her job much better if we sent her to a three-day conference at the Waldorf-Astoria in New York where she could network with an eye to developing some business for us. Foolishly, we did. She took her husband along and made a nice little vacation of it, at our expense. When she returned, her debriefing to me was all about the food, the accommodations, the Broadway plays she and her husband attended, and so forth. She said nothing about the meetings. When I grilled her on whom she had met and spoken to about our business, she was remarkably vague. Not a single one of her alleged marketing efforts during the meeting bore any fruit whatsoever.

139. DON'T CONDUCT PERSONAL BUSINESS ON THE JOB

I worked at the Pentagon for several years and was astounded by the number of full-time Defense Department employees—both military and civilian lawyers included—who were very ably supplementing their government salaries with side businesses. Side businesses, I should add, that were being run out of their Pentagon offices on company time, using government resources (telephones, desks, supplies, equipment, etc.), and all being done rather overtly and shamelessly.

My first day at work, a full colonel in the air force called me into his office and pulled out a poster displaying a variety of dress and casual shoes that he wanted me to buy. Later that day, a civilian attorney in my office asked me if I had considered whether to rent or buy a house. Naively, I answered her question, whereupon she attempted to sign me up as one of her real estate clients! When I declined, I made a permanent enemy, which did not serve me well down the line.

Some of these parallel-career businesses were, to say the least, exotic: a colonel who sold specialty pickles on the side; another colonel who ran what I can only describe as a religious Ponzi scheme, having purchased an "archbishopric" with authority to sell "bishop" designations to gullible individuals who would then recruit "ministers."

Another time during my first year on the job, a colleague asked me if I would like to collaborate with him on his next coffee-table book (I did not know he was an author). Flattered, I stupidly agreed, only to discover that he expected me to do the research at the Pentagon Law Library during working hours! I declined the offer . . . and made another enemy.

Why, you may reasonably ask, didn't anyone complain to the bosses? Simple. The bosses were doing it, too! In fact, the big boss, our division director, was the worst abuser of all, utilizing not only government property, but also federal employees during work time to run his very successful side business. For reasons I've never fully fathomed, he was able to get away with it for years. Years later at a wedding, I met a famous syndicated columnist who wrote investigative pieces and exposes, several of which were devoted to my division director. He could not explain how this cheating bureaucrat did it, either.

While that was the most extreme example I have ever encountered, this kind of stuff goes on all the time, and government employees snookering taxpayers are hardly the only culprits. Every time it happens, it is inexcusable. When I discovered it in my own organization, I ended it quickly by terminating the employee without notice, severance, or anything else.

140. DON'T DO ANYTHING IN PRIVATE YOU WOULD NOT DO IN PUBLIC

We launched a new subsidiary company in order to develop a promising sideline business—legal career transition counseling—to supplement our successful legal career publishing venture. Consequently, we hired an individual to administer the new subsidiary, and set him up in an office suite that we leased that was several floors away from our main office.

Shortly after he began working, I heard troubling tales from his secretary to the effect that she had walked into his private office in order to give him a message and caught him with his pants off. Needless to say, the story she told was disturbing and made me watch him more closely. It was not long before his bad behavior and bad judgment forced us to fire him.

Note that his employment difficulties began with conduct that he believed was private. Nothing in a workplace environment is ever totally private. If you engage in weird practices behind closed doors, someone will surely uncover them, and you will carry around a "Mark of Cain" for the rest of your days in that work environment, if not beyond.

The place to act kinky is not at work. This principle applies particularly to Internet abuse, which is rampant throughout the workplace. Don't do it.

141. DON'T KEEP A RADIO OR TV ON
YOUR DESK

One day I had to hand-deliver an information tax return to the U.S. Department of Labor headquarters in downtown Washington. When I walked into the appropriate office, the receptionist told me to wait until the soap opera she was watching went to a commercial. I cooled my heels for the next 10 minutes while she stared raptly at the TV screen on the corner of her desk. It was a surreal scene.

During my wait, my mind raced with confused thoughts: Was this representative of my government at work? Could it be that my tax dollars were actually paying this lady's salary and benefits? Was this the way for a public servant to behave? Should I take to the hills with a weapon, exhume Che Guevara, and start a revolution? Should I move to New Zealand?

Once the commercial interrupted her concentration on what was truly important in her life, she grumpily accepted my proffered information return and changed channels to another soap that was not at commercial.

By the time I returned to my office, I was obsessed with researching this strange encounter further. After several pass-along phone calls to government offices, I was advised to examine the collective bargaining agreement between the Labor Department and its workers. I managed to secure a copy of this public record in short order and discovered that radios and TVs were not only countenanced, but were actually *encouraged* by the agreement. Now this was really getting strange!

I followed up my discovery by seeking out an explanation from the department's public affairs office, which informed me that the agency's philosophy was that its workers be covered by the most progressive labor agreement possible, so as to serve as a model for the businesses that the agency regulated. No thank you.

The moral of this sad tale of taxpayer abuse is this: even if this kind of behavior is condoned by your employer, do not permit yourself to be tempted to do it. You will notice very quickly that none of the employees who get promoted to upper levels engage in this kind of employee abuse, despite its authorization by (mis)management.

142. DON'T LEAVE STUFF LYING AROUND THAT YOU DON'T WANT OTHERS TO SEE

Two anecdotes drive this point home like a stake through the heart:

In the first incident, I came into my office early one morning, went through my usual routine turning on lights, revving up the coffee machine, listening to overnight phone messages, and so forth. When I turned on the copy machine, I discovered a printed copy in the feeder tray. It was a flyer advertising a business venture that was clearly being conducted by one of our employees.

Now that is not so terrible in itself, although it would be dismaying to any employer to discover that (1) an employee was using office equipment clandestinely and (2) that she was obviously not intending to be around forever. But under the circumstances, this was the missing piece of a puzzle that had been bothering me for some time. I had not been able to figure out why we seemed to have experienced a surge in copying costs, postage meter costs, paper costs, and so forth. Now it became apparent. It was because this lady was stiffing us, using our supplies and equipment for her own personal purposes.

I wished her well and Godspeed with her new endeavor, her tenure with my company having ended when she walked in the door that morning.

The second illustration involves one of our legal career counseling clients who came to us with the following story: One evening he left work in a hurry and, inadvertently left his freshly minted résumé on his desk. The next morning there was a Post-it note attached to the résumé asking him to come see the boss immediately. The boss told him he was fired. Reason: He felt insulted that one of his loyal employees would be secretly seeking other employment.

Bosses are like that.

143. DON'T STEAL FROM YOUR EMPLOYER

In my first job out of law school working as a Pentagon attorney, I was invited by my coworkers on occasion for dinner at their homes. Invariably, I would see an array of office equipment at their houses—pens that said PROPERTY OF THE U.S. GOVERNMENT, for example—that had been lifted from the office. My thoughts would always turn to the question: what if the boss had been invited instead of me?

Taking home office supplies and equipment is theft, unless, of course, you take it home for the sole purpose of using it on behalf of the business. Otherwise, just say no. And don't try to justify this behavior by rationalizing that everyone does it. Honest people do not do it. Moreover, other ways of stealing from one's employer—for example, stealing time at work to run your own affairs—should also be avoided.

Don't appropriate office equipment for personal use. This should go without saying, but office theft by employees has become a multibillion-dollar problem according to the folks who monitor such discouraging statistics. Even if everyone around you were a "moral neuter," that would not be a reason to abandon your ethics and your sense of right and wrong. If you get caught—and be assured that your bosses are not completely ignorant of what happens to supplies and equipment—your job and your career can go into the tank very quickly.

If you want to use an office computer in order to prepare your brother's résumé, ask permission first, and then use it during off hours. If you need to use the postage meter for personal mail, ask permission, then reimburse petty cash.

144. DON'T LEAVE EQUIPMENT ON AT NIGHT

Every night I went around my company's office turning off computers, printers, air-conditioning units, and lights. Leaving this equipment on may or may not be bad for it (there are arguments both ways with regard to computers), but it does waste a nonrenewable resource (electricity), and someone (landlord or tenant) has to foot the bill for it.

145. DON'T ABUSE PHONE PRIVILEGES

An employee once came into my office, closed the door, and registered the following telephone-related complaints:

- He could get a lot more substantive work done if he did not have to answer the telephone all the time and take orders from customers. I reminded him that answering the phone and taking customer orders is (1) part of the job description that was explained to him when he interviewed for the job and then again when he first came to work and (2) the most important thing we do, since it represents our direct contact with our customers.
- Other individuals assigned to answer the telephone were not pulling their weight compared to him. When I pressed him to name names, he cited a former employee who had left three months before.

What he did not say was that he spent a good portion of every day making personal phone calls to family and friends. That day alone, for example, I counted five—when I was paying attention. This was inexcusable and he was warned that if he did not cut back on his personal calls, he would not be retained. He did and he was. But his gripe made me view him a bit differently than before.

This is the flip side of telephone etiquette. An office is not a place for socializing over the phone. You are not on your own time. In addition to limiting your outgoing calls to friends and family, advise them not to bother you at work unless there is an emergency.

Finally, it goes without saying that long distance calls are out of the question. If you have to make one, ask for permission and reimburse the employer.

This is a slight digression, but the point is important: Don't be so obtuse that you go to your boss and whine about something as unimportant as this. He or she will surely remember you in an unfavorable light.

146. DON'T PUT ANYTHING INTO AN EMAIL OR ON A SOCIAL NETWORK THAT COULD CAUSE TROUBLE

Emails and social networking websites like Facebook, Twitter, and LinkedIn have become the bane of legal (and many other) offices, and the downfall of a growing number of attorneys and other employees. The harm that such a record can produce can be not only job threatening, but business threatening as well.

Employers across the board have become almost paranoid about the damage an email can inflict on their organizations. Several of my disability insurance company clients now have a policy that absolutely precludes communicating with them via email about a case referral. Those client companies that still permit such emails instruct me not to mention the name of the insured in the email and to be very circumspect about what I say.

Since business emails are generally discoverable documents in lawsuits, the problems that emailing employees pose to their employers have escalated to toxic levels. A 2007 survey revealed that the average employee sends and receives 170 emails per day and resorts to his or her personal email account(s) for business purposes at least twice a week. Moreover, the more telecommuting increases (and it is increasing quite rapidly across America), the more likely employees who work from home are to use their personal email accounts for business.

Since personal emails are deemed discoverable by many courts, the potential legal exposure to businesses is enormous.

Another very good reason to exercise extreme care with your emails is because, regardless of what you assume, employers often do have access to your email accounts and will read them. The same holds true of social networking sites. Worse, your enemies could post things about you on these sites that are embarrassing, untrue, vicious, or vindictive (see also principle 221).

147. DON'T "OVERENGINEER"

Too many computer logs, desk calendars, date books, etc. can bog you down and quickly make you so obsessed with planning that actually performing the items on your multiple lists takes second place. In short, all of this organizing can often become an end in itself and risks the danger of substituting planning for performance. It can also delude you into thinking that checking something off on your to-do list is the equivalent of accomplishing an important task.

One way to avoid this is to limit yourself to only the planning tool(s) you need to be comfortably efficient. One date book for your personal life and a comparable device for your professional tasks is enough for most of us.

148. DON'T BE A YES PERSON

No one likes a sycophant (read: bootlicker or brownnoser). If you have an opposing opinion, and it is a well-reasoned one, your colleagues and bosses will respect you much more if you share it with them.

149. DON'T DRESS LIKE A HOLLYWOOD STAR

You may walk around with a see-through blouse at home, but work is definitely not the place for provocative garb. Sure, you will become famous, but for the wrong reasons. Despite all the talk about going casual and dress-down days, the old conservative standards of dress still control many legal workplaces, and most of the people at the top of the organizational heap still think traditional clothing is a must or at least a very good idea.

Dressing appropriately is a very small price to pay for job security.

150. DON'T INDULGE IN "WEEKEND ABUSE"

I lost count long ago of the number of days lost at my company by virtue of employees calling in on Monday morning to say that they (1) ate or drank something they should not have over the weekend and were too sick to make it to work, (2) returned from a weekend trip very late Sunday night and were too tired to come to work, or (3) . . . you get the picture.

Do what you want on your own time, but not if it is going to affect your ability to work on Monday. You owe a responsibility to your employer to show up for work on Monday morning—in a condition to be able to perform up to expectations.

In my experience, this kind of conduct is not only restricted to weekends. I also saw it during the week. This is no different than weekend abuse. You owe it to your employer to think about the impact of your evening on the next day at work.

Leading an exemplary, moderate life out of the office will ensure that you never make this mistake.

151. DON'T ABUSE YOUR BENEFITS AND PERKS

If you have an expense account, don't treat it as a license to kill. If you take (or are given) a $10 bill out of petty cash for a cab ride across town that winds up actually costing $5, return the change to the person who gave you the original amount.

If you have not yet earned vacation time, don't take it. Don't feign illness. It is surprising how many employees get sick on Thursday or Sunday night.

152. DON'T LOSE PERSPECTIVE ON WORKPLACE RELATIONSHIPS

The advice that follows, which in a nutshell is basically to keep your distance from your coworkers, may appear somewhat counterintuitive. After all, for many of us, work is the basis of our social relationships.

I do not mean to say that you should not be friendly with the people with whom you work. If you aren't, work will not be a lot of fun, and your attitude and even your productivity will suffer from isolation. However, you need to be wary in approaching each situation and judging each potential relationship on its own merits.

The contemporary workplace is a very different one from that which prevailed before. People change jobs much more often, moving from department to department within the same organization, as well as from one employer to another, with increasing frequency. The giant company that purchased my businesses reorganized at least three times between the date of purchase and the end of my employment and consulting contracts with it. With the growth of suburbs and exurbs and improved urban transportation systems, employees often do not live in the same communities where they work, a striking change from the past. Consequently, there is not as much opportunity for developing close relations and social friendships with coworkers.

The decline of social interaction among coworkers is not altogether a bad thing. In an era of constant and continuing downsizing, reorganization, restructuring, reengineering, reductions in force, and the like, it becomes a little more dangerous to develop such close relations that you share your secrets and your misgivings with your fellow employees. Many of them may be competing with you in the near future for job retention. The temptation to stab you in the back may be too much to resist.

153. DON'T CONFIDE IN YOUR COWORKERS

This is closely related to the preceding point. One of my legal career counseling clients lost his job because he confided in his best friend at work about his desire to seek new employment elsewhere. The best friend immediately went to the boss and told him the confidence. The boss was insulted that my client would even consider such a traitorous act. My client was fired.

Be careful in whom you confide or what you reveal about yourself to coworkers. Remember that they, like you, owe their first loyalty to your employer.

The best policy is to assume that you have no best friends at work.

154. DON'T HAVE INTIMATE RELATIONSHIPS WITH YOUR COWORKERS

Playing "kissy-face" at the office might be the beginning of kissing your job good-bye. Sexual relationships with coworkers are always detrimental to your job and your career. Stay away from them.

155. DON'T SHARE INTIMATE INFORMATION ABOUT YOURSELF

One of my counseling clients decided to announce at a companywide meeting that she had left her husband and moved in with her lesbian lover, who happened to be one of her coworkers (she publicly named the person!). She felt compelled to make that announcement because it was the "honest thing to do."

Within weeks her company found a way to terminate her employment for violating a corporate nonfraternization policy, among other things.

While some readers may recoil in horror at this corporate example of political incorrectness, that is irrelevant. The reality was that this young woman lost a well-paying job due to her urge to reveal things about her personal life that were nobody's business.

156. DON'T EXPLOIT PEOPLE

Your reputation is your most valuable commodity. If you go around the office taking advantage of your colleagues or the support staff, or "putting one over" on the boss, you will quickly develop a poor reputation. Others will, quite correctly, perceive you as untrustworthy and your credibility will diminish rapidly. This will do nothing for your job security.

157. DON'T IRRITATE YOUR BOSS OR COWORKERS

There are innumerable ways you could do this: by gabbing all day long, by talking to your friends on the telephone during work hours, by being perceived as not pulling your weight, by playing computer games when you should be working. The list of possibilities for ticking people off is virtually endless.

It is not only bosses who get upset by this kind of behavior. Every other diligent employee will also not take kindly to it. And they will become your worst enemies. Moreover, word of your inappropriate conduct will probably get back to a higher authority.

Don't rely for a moment on your boss being clueless as to your activities. As we mentioned earlier, I once employed someone who was attempting, clandestinely, to run her own moonlighting business from my office. Only it was hardly moonlighting, since she was doing it during working hours.

When I noticed that she began coming into the office early, purportedly to catch up on her work, I was impressed. However, when I discovered the flyer she forgot in the copy machine advertising her side business (containing our office phone number!), I was less impressed.

Another example of behavior guaranteed to irritate your boss is interrupting him or her with a less-than-pressing issue at a time you know to be very busy.

"I know how busy you are today, but . . ."

If you *know* your boss is busy, keep quiet about your problem or issue until he or she is *not* busy. I do not understand why so many employees decide that the perfect moment to bring up an issue that could easily wait is when the boss is under severe deadline pressure (and the employee knows it!). Bosses don't forget things like that easily. It becomes a lasting memory.

158. DON'T IGNORE YOUR OWN
ANNOYING HABITS

Virtually everyone has an annoying habit or two. Maybe you gnaw the nonbusiness end of pens. Or you don't wash your hands after using the bathroom facilities (some men seem to revel in this). A little self-analysis will tell you what these habits are.

They may be both personal and professional. If you are able to pinpoint your annoying habits, make an effort to correct them. Petty irritations like these add up and might be remembered when important decisions about your future are under consideration.

159. DON'T GET INTO FIGHTS WITH
YOUR COWORKERS

One of the attorneys in my office once chose the worst possible deadline-pressure day to go ballistic with someone else in the office she felt had been systematically slighting her. Talk about a bad moment! Everyone was heavily distracted the rest of the day (she launched her verbal missiles early in the morning), and the deadline project suffered as a consequence.

This is a surefire way to guarantee your dismissal in a downsizing, if not before. You will be perceived as a troublemaker, as well as someone who simply doesn't care about the important work of your organization.

Legal and other organizations abhor aggressive internal behavior—except when they are ridding themselves of someone for displaying it.

If you have a serious dispute with a colleague, try to resolve it out of the office, or take it to the boss for resolution. If you have difficulty getting along with another person in your office, get over it! Keep your relationships with those you dislike on a purely professional level and everything should be fine.

160. DON'T SHARE COMPENSATION INFORMATION

Keep your compensation and other matters that are no one else's business to yourself. Of course, in public sector employment, everyone knows what everyone else is earning, because those figures are published and are public information. Such intelligence is quite another matter in the private sector. Sharing what you make with your colleagues can be very distracting and can cause resentment that could come back to haunt you at a later time.

161. DON'T FIGHT CHANGE . . . WELCOME IT

Change is inevitable in any organization, so why fight it? It's going to happen, anyway. Your best strategy is to anticipate it, plan for how you might fit in to it, and finally, embrace it.

Most of your coworkers will resist change, be mightily distracted by it, and will leave a bad taste in the mouths of the change promoters. You, in contrast, will shine by comparison.

162. DON'T REST ON YOUR ACADEMIC LAURELS

Every employer nowadays knows how suspect academic grades have become, after many years of grade inflation and teachers' fears of calling anyone a failure. I have had English majors, journalism majors, and attorneys from top schools and with grade point averages in the stratosphere who could not string two coherent and grammatically correct sentences together.

When Stanford University eliminates failing grades; when studies show that over 80 percent of all college grades in the United States are either A's or B's; when the Scholastic Aptitude Test (SAT) decides it has to re-center its averages because of the precipitous decline in test scores; when 88 percent of the graduates of a great university graduate with honors compared to 8 percent a decade before—employers have naturally begun to discount high grades.

The only thing that counts is present and future performance. Your success in school cannot compensate for your failure on the job. The great schools on your résumé will only get you so far. Being an alum of Yale College and Harvard Law School is a great accomplishment and likely will open many doors for you in your career and your life, but it quickly becomes yesterday's news. Ultimately, performance on the job is what counts.

I have handled hundreds of outplacement clients who graduated from top schools with top honors, only to find themselves in front of me because they had been terminated by their law firms, corporations, government agencies, and nonprofits for poor performance or a less tangible lack, such as a poor attitude or an inability to fit in.

Your academic achievements are a wonderful platform, but they are not enough to triumph in the working world.

163. DON'T TAKE IT PERSONALLY IF SOME OF YOUR SUGGESTIONS ARE NOT ADOPTED

I had an employee once who descended into a deep and long-standing sulk if every single one of her ideas was not immediately adopted and implemented. It got so bad that she would stop speaking to the rest of the office staff for days at a time. Naturally, when a decision had to be made whether to retain her, we decided that, despite her occasionally good ideas and her good work habits, we did not need her.

All ideas have to go through a vetting process in order to prove themselves worthy. Don't agonize over this process. It is not intended as a personal attack on the suggester. Rather, it is part of the difficult corporate decision-making process through which it is determined to put company money behind an innovation.

If your ideas get rejected from time to time, pick your ego up, dust it off, and come up with new and improved suggestions. Analyze why your idea did not survive to the implementation stage and use this knowledge to build a better mousetrap.

Bosses are not only impressed with successful ideas. They are also positively influenced by the fact that someone in the organization has taken the initiative and come up with a suggestion. Simply proposing a new idea builds capital with your employer.

164. DON'T TAKE CLIENT ABUSE PERSONALLY

Irate clients are as inevitable as death and taxes. If you are in the legal world long enough, you will be sure to run into a slew of unreasonable, if not hysterical, clients. These days, when every client seems to demand customization, the likelihood of running smack into an angry one is quite high.

I had my share of supersensitive employees who seemed to think that every encounter with an angry client was a personal attack on them. Several of them became so enraged by such (rare) events that they became obsessed to the point of becoming ineffective at work. Their inability to distinguish personal from business assaults was factored into career decisions concerning them, such as promotions, raises, and terminations.

You are not the "u" in "us."

165. DON'T SPEAK ILL OF YOUR EMPLOYER, BOSSES, OR COWORKERS

Bad-mouthing someone sometimes appears to be the fuel of the modern workplace. When I took the subway to work in the morning and home at night, I was often the involuntary eavesdropping recipient of an endless barrage of complaints about on-the-job miseries and outrages, usually directed at the organization, the boss, or one or more coworkers. Most of these complaints, frankly, did not sound very justified. They were largely about rather petty and insignificant matters. People, it was easy to conclude, just like to complain and whine.

However, a loyal and discreet employee doesn't vent in this way. You never know who might be listening. It could easily be someone who could have a negative impact on your employer or on you, rather than a disinterested bystander.

There is another reason to behave properly. If everybody bitches and moans about everything all the time (which seems more and more the case), then you will stick out like a champion if you refrain from doing it.

166. DON'T BAD-MOUTH PAST EMPLOYERS

It is only common sense that employers tend to identify with other employers, not with employees. If you trash them, your employer undoubtedly thinks you probably feel the same way about him or her and are likely manifesting your contempt in public. Needless to say, that perception is hardly conducive to job security.

Job applicants who foolishly do this during job interviews—and I am always astounded at the many who do—don't realize that they are cutting their own throats. A legal job applicant who impressed me during her interview turned around just before leaving my conference room and said, "By the way, I should mention that I am suing my former employer."

End of being impressed.

167. DON'T MAKE VAGUE COMPLAINTS

If and when you have a serious criticism, make a private appointment with your boss, then come out and say it. Don't do what so many employees do and gripe indirectly: "Not everyone here is pulling his weight . . . " or "I've heard other (nameless) employees complaining about (a person) or (a policy)."

This kind of half-baked character assassination leaves a very bad taste in the employer's mouth. Nobody likes a snitch, a stoolie, or a confidential informant. Any TV police drama will tell you that.

Sure, your boss will be curious—perhaps even worried—about whether there is any truth to your allegations. Unfortunately for you, the boss's opinion of you will plummet, thanks to your gutless approach to the alleged problem.

If you do feel the need to go to your boss with a criticism or gripe, come in with a suggested solution, if at all possible. Don't leave your grievance hanging. Not only does a constructive, positive recommendation for improvement temper the grousing, it also adds value if it is implemented—both to your organization and to your boss's memory of your foresight and capabilities.

168. DON'T FORGET WHO SIGNS YOUR PAYCHECK

Never forget that your first loyalty in the workplace is to your organization. It provides you with your paycheck and your future opportunities. Your coworkers do not.

I once bought a large cache of office supplies at a distress sale of a major law firm that was closing its doors. Enough supplies, I felt, to more than adequately cover future office needs for many years to come. At the time, we had a satellite office on another floor in our building, manned by several professionals and one administrative employee. The administrative employee sat, closemouthed, while the professionals, systematically and in plain view, looted virtually all of the office supplies, taking home bags full of them for weeks. She never said a word until long after our satellite office was closed, the culprits long gone, and our operations consolidated in our main office.

I felt taken by the thieves and very badly served by the administrative employee who kept her mouth shut until long after the foxes had cleaned out the henhouse. Needless to say, her expendability quotient went up significantly from that day forward. After that, I never trusted her again, and it became only a matter of time until she left the organization, not wholly voluntarily.

Knowing that something untoward is going on in your organization and considering whether to report it to the authorities puts you in a very difficult position. Do you rat on your coworkers, or do you keep quiet and permit their abuses to continue unchecked? One way to resolve the situation would be to suggest to your colleagues that what they are doing is not appropriate and to recommend that they stop. In the supply anecdote above, it would certainly have been proper for the witness to the wrongdoing to suggest that the thieves return the items they took. This might accomplish two things: first, your conversation might actually stop the abuse; and second, there will be an implication in what you say to them that you might report the abuse to the boss if they don't stop.

Another way to handle this specific situation would be to inform the boss that you have noticed that the supplies were being used at a very rapid rate. Then, you will not have told on a colleague while, at the same time, you will have alerted your boss that the situation required examination.

169. DON'T ASK FOR A RAISE TOO SOON

Employers should reward people who are doing a good job. That philosophy often results in raises, sometimes within less than a year since the last raise. If you get the sense that you have landed in an organization like this, just relax. If you do a good job, raises will come your way—and may pleasantly surprise you in terms of their amount and frequency.

What is really annoying to employers—especially those who do watch out for their employees in this way—is someone who, having quite recently received a raise, promptly asks for another one. It makes the employer feel unappreciated and exploited. It also may poison the relationship for the future.

One of my employees once did this to me three months after receiving a handsome raise, basing her request on the grounds that she now had added responsibilities. While that was possibly true, her added duties did not require her to work any longer hours. She was still able to do her job within the context of our normal workweek. In other words, there was no justification for a raise at that time. Unfortunately, our denial of her request stimulated her desire to seek other employment and we lost a decent employee. No telling what she might have lost.

170. DON'T ASK FOR THE MOON

Closely related to asking for a raise too soon is asking for the moon. One of my employees once casually asked me, "How do you think I am doing?" I foolishly did not think through the implications of her seemingly offhand remark and replied, "Quite well. Keep up the good work."

The next day she asked me for a *40 percent raise!* Trying to maintain a poker face, I denied her request. Her response? "But you said I was doing great!"

After that episode, I viewed her in a different light . . . and I was *very* sparing with my praise.

171. DON'T TURN EVERY ISSUE INTO ARMAGEDDON

One of my bosses used to figuratively slap an opponent in the face with a glove every time he was frustrated or stymied. Every issue became a confrontation, often way out of proportion to its significance.

He soon developed a reputation for crying wolf and was no longer taken seriously. It got so bad that his boss stopped inviting him to important meetings.

His loss of credibility had a devastating effect on my immediate office. We were tainted by his "sins" and it took a long time to recover, even after his departure.

Pick your spots to make your stand. Save your last stands for the really major items. It is not worth extending yourself for an unimportant issue.

172. DON'T MAKE EXCUSES OR BLAME OTHERS

If you screw up, be accountable. Take the blame. Learn your lesson and don't make the same mistake twice.

If something is your fault, accept it like a mature adult. Don't point the finger at others, like so many of our politicians do whenever things don't go their way or they think they can garner another vote by pinning something (true or untrue) on somebody else.

I cannot forget the precise moment when I completely lost respect for a political candidate who was making a serious run at a presidential nomination. He was campaigning in Illinois when a reporter asked him about a rather sleazy attack ad his campaign was running on television in another part of the country. The candidate immediately denied all knowledge of the ad and blamed it on one of his staffers. Whether he, in truth, knew nothing about the ad (which is rather hard to believe), he was the responsible party, but his character was such that he did not see it that way. For shame.

Be a *mensch*. Not a politician.

173. DON'T TELECOMMUTE UNLESS YOU HAVE NO CHOICE

Telecommuting is the wave of the future. Commuters in places like Los Angeles and the Washington, D.C., area, havens of commuting nightmares, dream of being able to work from home.

Don't do it.

While immensely attractive at first glance, telecommuting has proven to be dangerous to careers. To become truly indispensable, you need to be visible. Employers have found that it is much easier to lay off or fire someone they never see than it is to let go the people with whom they interact closely every day.

The only exception to this is an extremely rare one: if you are an attorney for an organization that judges you by your production and you are a big producer, then telecommuting becomes more possible. The U.S. Patent and Trademark Office (PTO) permits its trademark examining attorneys to telecommute, only rarely requiring their presence in the office. PTO is also one of the handful of legal organizations that is able to measure its attorneys' productivity accurately, in its case by the number of trademark applications per year processed to completion by each attorney. Attorneys who exceed the average by a certain percentage are rewarded with bonuses. Those who underperform might find themselves out of a job. Overachieving trademark examining attorneys are valuable employees and not likely to be in job jeopardy despite being tele-commuters. Another factor making this situation unique is that virtually every single attorney telecommutes. Consequently, they are all on equal footing.

Chapter 5

Personal Growth = Professional Growth

*C*HAPTERS 1 THROUGH 4 *focused on the steps necessary to secure your professional career. Chapter 5 takes a different approach, concentrating on the things you can do to grow as a person, all of which will enhance your professional persona.*

In addition to improving yourself professionally, you cannot and should not ignore your personal side. You will find that, very often, the two are quite complementary and synergistic. The initiatives to improve yourself that you undertake outside of work will enhance your work product and relationships and help you to become more indispensable to your employer.

There is much that you can do, and do efficiently, to add value both to your own life and to your work performance. Virtually anything you do to improve your communication skills will help you grow professionally. This is perhaps more central to success as an attorney than in almost any other

profession. Attorneys must be able to communicate clearly and unambigu-
ously to colleagues, clients, judges, witnesses, opposing counsel, etc.

Reading, writing, and speaking are relatively easy and seamless ways
to improve these skills and to achieve the most carryover from the personal
to the professional.

174. READ CONSTANTLY

Reading not only gives you immensely valuable information that may come in handy on the job, it is also wonderful relaxation and an overall good time. In addition, it will make you a much better communicator, both orally and in writing, than your colleagues who spend much, if not all, of their leisure time watching television and/or surfing the Internet.

I derive a great many of my best ideas from the associations I make through reading eclectically. I even glean some great ideas from fiction. I never read without a notebook nearby to jot down interesting thoughts that are triggered by the content.

175. WHAT TO READ: HISTORY AND BIOGRAPHY

Well-written history and biography are some of the best-kept secrets of our—or any—time. They are mostly literate, informative, and above all, tremendously instructive. In short, they are essential to a well-rounded individual who wants to learn from the past while being exposed to good writing.

President Harry Truman, an entirely self-educated man, was a voracious reader of history and biography. He was also one of our most successful chief executives, and he himself attributed his achievements primarily to his lifelong habit of reading history and biography.

There is a saying:

> *"Those who cannot remember the past are*
> *condemned to repeat it."*

While this is a fundamental precept of my life, I would take it a step further. Call it Hermann's Corollary to George Santayana (the author of the above quotation):

> *"Those who do not learn from the successes of the past*
> *are missing out on easy victories."*

In other words, you can learn two very valuable things from what went on in the past: what went wrong, but also what went right.

176. WHAT TO READ: ECONOMIC HISTORY

The best way to get this point across is to identify several recurring phenomena of very recent economic history:

- The real estate boom of the late 1970s followed by the real estate bust of the early 1980s and real estate's turnaround in the mid-1980s. In 1978, my wife and I were house hunting during a period when house prices in our area were skyrocketing. Houses were selling almost as quickly as they came on the market and often for more than the asking price! Amazed and somewhat intimidated, we wondered if it might be better to wait a bit before buying. With this in mind, I kept posing the question to real estate agents: "When is all this craziness going to end?"

"Never," replied the agents uniformly. "This boom will continue as far out as the eye can see, so now is the time to buy, before prices go even further through the roof."

Guess what? The bottom fell out of the market a year later, and houses that sold for $X could be had for $X minus 15 percent. The same thing happened again a few years later, with the same overly enthusiastic responses from realtors, and unfortunately, with the same results. The market collapsed, leaving lots of folks who had bought at the peak holding monstrous mortgages that often exceeded the value of their properties.

Both recent real estate boom-and-bust cycles were completely forgotten during the latest and greatest real estate boom, the one that began in the late 1990s and went all the way to 2007 before going into a death spiral of historic proportions. Anyone conversant with the cyclical nature of the real estate market could have predicted both the bust and, with some degree of accuracy, the timing of the beginning of the downturn. There was a flood of good books and online information (see, e.g., the Case-Schiller U.S. Home Price Indices at *www.metroarea.standardandpoors.com*) available on the subject that should have been required reading for anyone involved in the market.

- The "New Economy," made manifest by dot-com companies. These companies had no apparent business model and no hope of ever achieving profitability, but had plenty of dupes lining up to throw their venture capital and retirement funds at them in hopes of a quick kill. We were told by all of the experts that this time the economy would operate quite differently and that we had better hop on the bandwagon before it ran past us. They might have been right about hopping on, but they sure blew it when it came to hopping off. The New Economy proved to be not so new after all and to be governed by the same timeless rules as the Old Economy it purportedly replaced.

Again, it was all there in books and articles (see, e.g., "Dotcoms Get the Spotlight, Old Economy Gets the Dough," *Video Age International* (July 28, 2005)) for anyone with curiosity to discover.

- The Great Recession. This is my label for the current economic difficulties that plague us and that will be with us for a very long time. It did not take much in the way of brains or perceptiveness to realize that financial exotica such as subprime mortgages, instantaneous securitization of these dangerous loans, collateral debt obligations, and credit default swaps, to name a few, were going to blow up in someone's face. Actually, in all of our collective faces.

The economy, whether new or old, local, domestic, or global, follows principles that have governed it since *Homo erectus* came down from the trees. Knowing that will already give you an immense advantage over everyone who is ignorant enough to believe something else.

You could have known all of that if you had read economists like Adam Smith (*The Wealth of Nations*), John Maynard Keynes (especially *The End of Laissez-Faire; The Economic Consequences of the Peace*), Charles Beard (*An Economic Interpretation of the Constitution of the United States*), Milton Friedman (especially *Capitalism and Freedom*), John Kenneth Galbraith (*The Great Crash; The Affluent Society*), Paul Krugman (especially *The Return of Depression Economics; The Great Unraveling: Losing Our Way in the New Century*), Robert Schiller (*Subprime Solution*), or my all-time favorite, Charles MacKay (*Extraordinary Popular Delusions and the Madness of Crowds*). Keynes excepted, all pretty easy and entertaining reads, by the way. And all invaluable to any aspiring economic participant.

177. WHAT TO READ: SELECTED SELF-IMPROVEMENT BOOKS

There is a lot of literature available on almost every facet of running your life, from organizing the clutter in your closet to playing tiddlywinks like a professional to attracting the opposite sex without the intervention of pheromones. A quick glance at the table of contents, the credibility of the author, and a scan of several pages will quickly tell you if a particular book might be one worth examining further.

If you glean one nugget of wisdom out of a self-improvement book, one idea you can run with in your personal life or work, the read will have been worth it.

To give yourself the greatest benefit, stick with reality in your self-improvement reading. Stay away from silly stuff like psychic predictions, astrology, alchemy, and opportunistic jottings with cute, catchy titles like *Learn to Pillage the Genghis Khan Way*.

A few of the best books in this genre are John C. Maxwell (*Failing Forward: Turning Mistakes into Stepping Stones for Success*), Janet Elsea (*First Impression, Best Impression*), Steven R. Covey (*The 7 Habits of Highly Effective People*), and Susan Jeffers (*Feel the Fear and Do It Anyway*).

178. WHAT TO READ: ABOUT WINNERS . . . AND LOSERS (AND LOSERS WHO BECAME WINNERS)

Reading about people, organizations, countries, etc. who won big and lost big can be very instructive. From the former, e.g., Barack Obama, Google, the United States, you can learn a lot about the secrets of their success. You know, for example, all those stirring speeches of Winston Churchill during World War II, speeches that were full of powerful words and phrases that rallied an almost-defeated people to eventual victory:

"We shall fight on the beaches. We shall fight in the cities.
We shall fight in the towns and villages . . .
We shall never surrender . . ."

and

"It was their finest hour . . ."

and

"Neither blood nor sweat nor toil nor tears . . ."

Great stuff! It all sounded so spontaneous and unrehearsed. Well, every single one of those speeches that moved a nation, that looked to the eyes of Churchill's fellow members of Parliament and sounded to all the millions listening around their radios like brilliant extemporaneous utterances were in fact rigorously planned and rehearsed. They were refined to the point that they appeared completely spontaneous!

You can learn an immensely valuable lesson from this insight. Remember, however, when you are studying successful people, that it is their successes you want to emulate and attempt to incorporate into your program for self-improvement. You want to absorb the best of their characters and role modeling . . . and discard the rest.

Similarly, you can learn an awful lot about how *not* to conduct yourself from reading about the big losers. A spate of good books, for example, are available about some of the spectacular governmental and business failures of our (and earlier) times. The government-nurtured collapse of the savings and loan industry, the demise of IBM during the 1980s, the fall of the Wall Street high fliers of the 80s, and the collapse of Enron, for example, are all well documented in literature and are as instructive in their own way as the inspiring books about Winston Churchill.

Losers who turn their lives around and become winners are perhaps the most inspiring of all. Churchill was the guiding spirit behind one of the greatest achievements of mankind, but he was also the architect of Gallipoli in World War I, one of the bloodiest and most colossal military disasters of the 20th century. He spent 20 years in the political wilderness before being recalled to greatness.

Abraham Lincoln lost two Illinois Senate races (1854 and 1858). He was devastated, especially by the latter defeat, but he learned from his mistakes and went on to the presidency only two years later.

The point is to read this material and to keep up with what is being written about winners and losers. Again, if you come away with just one useful idea out of each of these books, you will be light-years ahead of your peers.

179. WHAT TO READ: FORWARD-LOOKING PUBLICATIONS

By forward-looking, I mean publications that (1) are well-respected leaders in their fields and (2) look ahead rather than merely reporting on what just happened. Several publications meet this test and are invaluable tools for indispensability:

- *The Economist* (*www.economist.com*). Nothing else in English comes close.
- *Technology Review* (*www.technologyreview.com*). MIT's coverage of cutting-edge technologies and their potential applications.
- *Wired* (*www.wired.com*). The best website of all the top publications.
- *Science News* (*www.sciencenews.org*). Keeps the layperson up-to-date on science matters.

- *The American Scholar* (*www.theamericanscholar.org*). Even the letters to the editor are informative.
- *The New York Review of Books* (*www.nybooks.com*). Book reviews are fine; think pieces are great.
- *National Journal* (*www.nationaljournal.com*). A must for every Washington insider and wannabe.
- *Legal Affairs* (*www.legalaffairs.org*). The law in real life.
- *Law Fuel* (*www.lawfuel.com*). Aggregates more than you might ever have wanted to know about law and lawyering.
- *Above the Law* (*www.abovethelaw.com*). Real-time reporting on legal career developments.

180. LOOK FOR OPPORTUNITIES TO WRITE

There will be few jobs in the Information Age that will not put a high premium on the ability to express oneself in writing. Perhaps because television viewing and Net surfing have largely replaced reading as the primary leisure activities of the world's population, the number of people who can write well is dwindling at the very moment the demand for them is increasing.

That gives you a tremendous window of opportunity. If you can develop good writing skills, you will have a significant leg up on the competition.

How do you develop good writing skills? In the old days, people used to communicate with each other primarily by writing letters. Thomas Jefferson wrote 9,000 letters during his life and made copies of most of them. Letter writing today is a lost art. It is so much easier and virtually effortless to pick up the phone and call someone or to sit down at your computer and plunk out a hasty email utterly lacking in either forethought or clear expression.

Virtually nobody writes snail-mail letters anymore. If you force yourself to write letters on a schedule, you will develop some of the good writing skills that you need. Email is normally no substitute for real letters. Most people don't put much effort into thinking about what they are going to write when they churn out an email. Of course, you could commit yourself to turning at least some of your emails into bona fide, lengthy, well-thought-out letters.

Another way to develop writing skills is to write and submit articles for publication. With tens of thousands of newspapers, journals, magazines, newsletters, and blogs around, articles on topics of interest to particular audiences are in great demand. You may not get paid, at least not initially, for your submissions, but that is not the point.

A very important collateral benefit of writing for publication is the positive publicity you earn from it. People think of you as an expert on the topic. You have something to point to on your résumé that distinguishes you from the crowd of applicants. And you may even cultivate your writing avocation into a traveling career, should the need to move on in the job market arise.

By the way, always get at least one reprint from the publication for which you are writing. Reprints make good promotional pieces for yourself.

You can also easily launch a blog. However, be very careful what you write about and the websites to which you link in your blog. Filter everything through the question "How would my employer view this?"

181. LOOK FOR PUBLIC SPEAKING OPPORTUNITIES

This is another way to establish yourself simultaneously as an expert and an energetic business developer while honing your oral communication skills. Your bosses will see you as more versatile. It is also a confidence builder that will help you in your professional environment.

Opportunities to speak publicly are all around you: Rotary clubs, Kiwanis clubs, other membership organizations . . . the list goes on and on. They need speakers for their luncheons and meetings. Develop an expertise and you become a natural for these gatherings. Moreover, once you develop a public reputation as an expert in a particular field, you won't have to aggressively seek out public speaking opportunities. Organizations in need of speakers will seek you out.

182. LEARN A LANGUAGE

Both the world and the U.S. economy have gone global. There won't be any turning back. It has become painfully obvious that the days of splendid isolation—and insulation—from the tribulations of the rest of the world are gone forever. No more hiding behind the blessed good fortune of abundant resources, of an endlessly prosperous domestic market enormous enough to satisfy any producer. No more sitting smugly on our island of plenty, our nearest competitors and enemies over 3,000 miles away across two vast oceans. The telecommunications, transportation, financial, and information revolutions have seen to that.

While English is the lingua franca of much of the economic and political activity of the world's nations, other countries and languages are also flexing their muscles. Almost half of the people in the world are either Chinese or Indian. Over a billion-and-a-quarter Chinese are rapidly becoming literate, energetic converts to the free market. It will be very difficult in the 21st century to ignore those numbers and that kind of economic clout. After almost 50 years of dithering flirtations with silly, otherworldly theories (like Third World Socialism), the very well-educated Indians have come around to the idea that they inhabit a tremendous market of potentially avid consumers, hard workers with middle class numbering in the hundreds of millions to act as the catalyst of a vibrant market economy.

German is suddenly a very important language, too. It is now the language of business not only in the German *Vaterland*, Austria, and portions of Switzerland, but also in much of Eastern Europe. If you want to make deals in Prague, Bratislava, Warsaw, Sofia, Budapest, Ljubljana, Bucharest, and even Kiev, German proficiency can be a huge help.

English also will not make the grade in the former Soviet Union, another large market with abundant natural resources, where Russian is the language of business and just about everything else, and the Russian people are years away from learning business English.

Americans have always had a quirky, isolationist attitude about foreign languages. I remember sitting in a lovely outside café in a small city in Germany years ago, watching in national embarrassment as a fellow American proclaimed loudly that he would be damned if he spoke anything other than English, and if the waiter didn't understand him, he could go shove his dessert pastries somewhere where the sun does not shine.

When I was stationed in Europe 25 years after the end of World War II, I was astounded at the few soldiers who took advantage of free, quality language courses. The typical American soldier assumed that the Germans and Italians ought to speak English if they wanted to get anywhere. They perceived it as an affront if anyone expected them to alter their ways, linguistically or otherwise.

Europeans have an advantage when it comes to learning languages. They live so close to one another that learning a language can be done with a rather easy trip over a nearby border. They learn languages by immersion. Americans, by contrast, are simply too far away from foreign language speakers to enjoy the same advantages.

As a people, we will never be able to change our casual language learning habits sufficiently to be on a par with our planetary competitors. I cannot imagine any kind of government educational policy that would reverse this laxity. Instead, like almost everything else in this land of rugged individualism, if you want to learn a language, you need to take the initiative yourself.

183. FIND AN EXTRACURRICULAR OUTLET FOR STRESS

These are highly stressful times, made more so by a suddenly uncertain world and problematic economic future. Many people leave work every day wound up as tight as drums.

We all need some sort of outlet where we can truly relax. A sport, a hobby, something. If you don't think you need one, you are not doing yourself a favor. You are also not doing your bosses, your coworkers, your family, your personal health, or your career a favor either.

Swimming is my release. When I develop a steady rhythm in the pool, I tend to loosen up and unwind. It is great physical therapy and psychotherapy.

Whether you run, swim, bike, row, collect stamps and coins, ballroom dance, play the zither, or something else, find something to do outside of work that is not work. This may not be an easy thing to do in the era of 24/7 ties to the office via email, your Blackberry, and your cell phone. But it is more important now than ever.

184. GIVE SOMETHING BACK

One of the most rewarding things you can do in life is to help someone else without worrying about being rewarded (in any external sense, monetary or otherwise) for your efforts. Volunteering is one of those rare activities that does not require posturing or prevaricating or any of the other unpleasant necessities that often attends work and virtually all other socioeconomic interaction.

On another level, you will be contributing something to the betterment of society, an endeavor that typically leaves the volunteer with a warm feeling of accomplishment.

Finally, we are fortunate to live in a remarkable country that allows us the freedom to pursue whatever we want and asks very little of us in our role as citizens in return. While we tend to take this kind of life for granted, it is extremely rare, both geographically and historically. In return for this unique opportunity and good fortune, we owe an unenforceable debt to the community. If you can make time and are not doing so already, begin now to repay it.

Notwithstanding the selfless quality of such activity, it can have a remarkably positive effect on one's career. Volunteer work looks very good on a résumé. It shows that you are not an idler, a couch potato who goes home every night and zones out in front of the TV set. It can also give you the opportunity to expand your horizons and learn new skills. While you may not have occasion to manage or supervise on the job, there are plenty of volunteer arenas where you can pick up such valuable experience. Finally, volunteering is a wonderful way to network, to build up a group of contacts who can be immensely helpful to you down the road.

In the interests of full disclosure, my wife and I have been volunteering since the first days of our marriage, primarily with respect to disabled and elderly Americans. In addition to being psychically rewarding on a grand scale, my volunteer work has translated into business opportunities. One consequence of my disability volunteering has been the opportunity to establish a unique subsidiary business: advising disability insurance companies on the issues they face involving attorneys who are receiving disability insurance benefits. Issues range from assisting disabled insured lawyers to return to work to advising the companies involved in disputes with benefits recipients.

This is a perfect example of how volunteer work can translate into expanded professional opportunities.

Chapter 6

The Legal Manager's Corner

*I*F YOU ARE SUCCESSFUL *and have become indispensable by applying the principles in chapters 1 through 5, chances are that someday you will find yourself promoted to a legal managerial position. Chapter 6 is devoted to the principles that legal managers must be cognizant of if they wish to shine as managers and continue to be indispensable.*

The advice in chapters 1 through 5 also applies to legal supervisors and managers to the same extent that it applies to other employees. In addition, legal managers have to cope with a whole plateful of issues that could ultimately impact their job security. Most of these concern how they cope with their staffs, and this is the primary focus of this chapter.

185. DON'T TAKE YOUR JOB DESCRIPTION AS GOSPEL

If you do, you may be surprised. The legal world is changing so rapidly that you cannot assume anything, including your duties when you tackle a new management position. Restructuring is the order of the day in the modern workplace. Between the time you were hired and the day you report to work, everything, agendas included, might have changed. The pace of change is accelerating. Industries and organizations are like hamsters on a treadmill, having to run faster and faster just to stay in place.

Law is no exception. In fact, the legal business may be more subject to change—and frequent change—than any other profession or industry. Congress enacts hundreds of new laws every year, while state and local legislatures enact thousands. The U.S. Supreme Court and Courts of Appeal, as well as their state counterparts, are constantly interpreting and reinterpreting the law. Add in the tens of thousands of regulations that are issued and revised each year, plus executive orders, administrative rulings, and directives, and you are confronted with the apotheosis of change. The only thing predictable about law is its unpredictability.

Factor in that we have now entered what appears to be a lengthy period of policy reversals and new policy initiatives, all of which must be memorialized by law, plus the sea changes affecting the way attorneys do business, and you can only conclude that managing in a legal environment has become a huge and daunting challenge.

If you want to succeed, much less survive, in this environment, you must be adaptable—as adaptable as a chameleon. If you don't, you may be operating under a set of assumptions that were bedrock gospel yesterday, but have already been consigned to history today and bear little relationship to the real-time world in which your performance and results will be judged.

Consequently, view your formal job description as a very general skeleton upon which it will be incumbent on you to add muscle, sinew, and nervous pathways.

186. DON'T CHANGE ANYTHING YET

When you begin your new job, keep an open mind. Develop your own opinions as to what must be done, based on the evidence, before going off half-cocked.

Managers tend to want to reorganize everything the minute they arrive. This was certainly my experience with management in every legal position I held. Reorganization, my attorney colleagues and I concluded, was the last bastion of a new manager who felt insecure and uncertain of how to proceed.

The best example of really bad behavior in this context is the political appointee who comes into his or her agency and immediately turns it upside down. This happens more often than not in Washington, D.C., to the detriment of agency and civil servant performance. The public pays a steep price every time this happens. Unfortunately, it happens almost every time there is a change of management. Morale plummets and even less gets accomplished than usual.

Resist the temptation to reorganize, or change anything else for that matter, when you first arrive on the job. Better to learn what the organization is all about before you tinker with it. Doing nothing dramatic or draconian at first will earn you valuable capital with the people who count the most: your staff.

187. DETERMINE IF AND WHY YOUR PREDECESSOR FAILED

This precept only applies if (1) you had a predecessor and (2) he or she quit, was fired, or left under some sort of cloud. You want to know as much as you can about the circumstances of the departure so that you don't reinvent the wheel and make the same mistakes. Naturally, you will have to be discreet about your inquiries.

Acquiring this kind of insight is invaluable and learning from it can be one of the critical keys to your success. Remember, succeeding where someone recently failed is a tremendous endorsement of your capabilities.

188. PINPOINT POTENTIAL PITFALLS

This is directly related to the point about determining if and why your predecessor failed. If you had to replace someone who did not retire of his or her own volition or did not leave in order to take another, more enticing position, then you know there was a problem. Otherwise, you would not have the job.

You want, at all costs, to avoid falling into the same trap(s). Learn from history. Don't repeat someone else's mistakes.

There is no better example of this than what is going on at the apex of American society. A new president is closely scrutinizing the failed policies of his predecessor and attempting to go a different path.

189. GET TO KNOW YOUR STAFF

Get to know your people, their jobs, their work habits, the quality of their work, and also their personalities and behavioral characteristics. You can also learn about their lives outside of work (without being intrusive). Privately, you may want to develop your own "profile" of them, a handy device when it comes to motivation, rewards, and discipline.

When I worked as an attorney at the Defense Department, the best manager that I ever encountered came into the position and immediately sat down individually with each attorney and other staff member in the office. My own meeting with him lasted a half-day and included a meal. He did not lay down any policies or rules of conduct or procedure for me. Rather, he listened, took some notes, probed deeply into my professional background, seemed genuinely interested in my personal story, and left me with the feeling that I would follow him into battle if called upon.

His tenure in the position was consistent with my initial meeting with him. When he left after 18 months, I and the rest of the staff were devastated.

190. UNDERSTAND THE BASICS OF EACH POSITION

Unless you understand what each of your staff members does, you cannot manage effectively. Developing this base knowledge requires more than reading every position description. Sit down with each employee and ask them what they do, how they do it, what they need to know in order to do their jobs, and what they might suggest to enable them to perform more efficiently and effectively.

Take notes. If someone recommends something that, upon reflection, you believe has merit, talk to your own supervisor(s) about implementing it. That is a great way to develop your credibility vis-à-vis your staff.

191. RADIATE CONFIDENCE

This is even more important in the supervisory context than for the employee. Remember, your staff is always watching you, just as you, presumably, are watching them. They will be alert to any chinks in your armor and will take advantage of them.

My army squad leader invariably did two self-defeating things that made him ineffective. First, he constantly demonstrated his indecisiveness, so much so that his squad members often had to cover for him. Second, and perhaps even worse, he too eagerly and obsessively sought the approval of his subordinates. That was clearly communicated to us as weakness, and we jumped all over the poor fellow for it. Suddenly, we became aware that we had a tremendous power over him: the power to withhold our approval. Once we had him labeled as a weakling, it was all over for him. His authority disappeared. We did what we wanted when we wanted. He became a nonfactor.

Employees in general have uncannily sensitive antennae when it comes to noticing signs of weakness in their bosses or coworkers. And once they detect it, there is almost no way to recover. Lawyers are particularly sensitive to any weaknesses, since their whole professional being revolves around probing for weakness in an opponent, a document, an argument, etc., in order to exploit it on behalf of their client. Understanding that this is a fact of legal life is crucial to your own managerial success.

You will almost certainly be tested by your staff. Never let them see you sweat, quiver, hesitate, or come across as uncertain.

192. CULTIVATE A POSITIVE, OPTIMISTIC ATMOSPHERE

People who feel good perform better than those who are down in the dumps. Morale is a critically important component of organizational success. Poor morale leads to poor performance and nonperformance.

Early in my career, I served as legal advisor to a very high energy senior Defense Department official. He was so enthusiastic and optimistic about the changes he wished to make in the one million–plus strong military force of which he was the civilian chief that, after every meeting I had with him, I felt elated and eager to get on with the task at hand. If he had asked me to, I would have run through a wall.

Emulating his infectious enthusiasm and can-do attitude about everything is probably an impossible ideal. But you should strive to inject your charges with enough eagerness and positive feedback that morale will not be a problem.

193. BE A WALK-AROUND MANAGER

Good legal managers don't sit all day at their desks. They spend more time on their feet than on their seat, moving around the office monitoring how things are going with their staffs, offering guidance, and perhaps more important, being visible.

This has a dual positive effect. First, it lets the staff know that you are genuinely interested in their work and in assisting with it. Second, it sends a message that slacking off is not something that the staff can do without being discovered.

194. EVERY MEETING SHOULD HAVE GOALS AND A PLANNED AGENDA

If you don't have a clear idea what your meeting is intended to accomplish, don't schedule it. A meeting is a complete waste of time without an objective that it aspires to achieve. If you have trouble coming up with one, forget about holding the meeting. That is the worst form of corporate "bootstrapping." You have much more important and productive ways to spend your valuable time. So does your staff.

Attorneys have a lot of work to do, and much of it is deadline work. Most of it also requires a great deal of forethought and planning, which requires privacy and an opportunity for quiet contemplation. Wasting staff time on meetings solely for the sake of holding a meeting will dampen enthusiasm, decrease productivity, and result in a loss of respect for you.

Moreover, don't hold meetings merely for the sake of demonstrating that some sort of activity is taking place. This is a notorious habit of bureaucracy, whether public or private sector, and is a phenomenal time-waster. If you cannot commit to paper and give advance notice of what is to be discussed, there is no reason to hold the meeting in the first place.

You will find that, not only will the requirement for goals and an agenda deter the "meeting-addicted," it will also make for smoother, more organized, shorter, and more productive meetings.

195. ALIGN YOUR OBJECTIVES TO THE ORGANIZATION'S

The worst situation you can find yourself in is if you discover that you are pulling in a different direction from that of your organization. That is a guaranteed way to fail.

One of my legal career counseling clients took a position as general counsel with a major manufacturing firm. As soon as she began working, she imposed her own agenda on her legal staff, one that had nothing whatsoever to do with the core mission of her employer, which was to maximize shareholder value and expand market share. Instead, she focused almost all of the legal department's attention on reviews of thousands of company documents—employment manuals, ethics and standard of conduct codes, safety guidelines, ongoing contracts, etc.—in order to identify and excise anything that met her definition of gender bias. "He" became "s/he" . . . you get the drift.

This task took months to accomplish, during which essential legal projects festered. It took the company CEO only a few days to terminate her employment once he became aware of the problems the legal department's delays had caused. This despite a corporate concern that she would initiate a gender discrimination claim if she were let go.

Find out as much as you can about organizational goals and then make sure that yours, as well as your department's, fall into line with the goals of the larger organization. At some point, it is inevitable that you will be measured by how closely your work comes to meeting company objectives.

196. MAKE YOUR HIGH EXPECTATIONS KNOWN

Demand a lot of your staff. Contrary to popular belief, you will discover to your satisfaction that people respond well to high performance expectations. If you don't believe this, think back to Vince Lombardi and the perennial champion Green Bay Packers of the 1960s. One of his players once said of him: "He treats us all equally . . . like dogs." While something of a bemused exaggeration, Lombardi to this day is revered by Packer alumni because he demanded much, and the results were the rewards of making it to the pinnacle of the profession.

Other examples abound, and not only in athletics. History is full of examples of military leaders who demanded peak performance of their troops and were rewarded for their approach by great victories and permanent places in history: Miltiades at Marathon; Leonidas at Thermopylae; Themistocles at Salamis; Alexander at Arbela; Hannibal at Lake Trasimene and Cannae; Charles Martel at Poitiers; William the Conqueror at Hastings; Marlborough at Blenheim; Nelson at Trafalgar; Napoleon at Austerlitz; Wellington at Waterloo; Spruance at Midway; Montgomery at Alamein; Zhukov at Stalingrad; Eisenhower at Normandy; MacArthur at Inchon.

Organizations are no different. Everyone wants to feel motivated by a cause. It is up to you as the leader to give your people one that will inspire them.

197. CULTIVATE ALLIES AND BUILD ALLIANCES

Forming alliances with colleagues is a good way to protect yourself and also learn about the organization. Your allies, with whom you can share information, will be able to serve as an early warning system as well as a brainstorming group and sounding board.

Allies can also support your program, but only if you earn their respect first by demonstrating both competence and consistency and showing them that you will be able to help them achieve their agendas, too.

Again, you can take a lesson from geopolitics. President George H. W. Bush crafted a global alliance to support the liberation of Kuwait in Desert Storm in 1991. President George W. Bush ignored his father's wise precedent when he invaded Iraq in 2003, with decidedly different results. When his administration went into the tank, there was no one left in the world to support him.

198. DELEGATE

This is critical for legal supervisors. Many successful people who work their way up the ladder of a law organization cannot seem to let go. They feel that they have to be in control of everything. For a time, perhaps, they are able to do their jobs and maintain their status in the organization. However, eventually, as they are saddled with additional responsibilities or simply amass more work to do, they run into trouble, still attempting to be all things to all people.

This stressed-out approach is eventually going to get to anyone who tries to live like this. Ultimately, they will fail.

It is both reckless and risky to attempt to do everything yourself. This mentality is a trap that has destroyed many legal managers.

You simply have to force yourself to get out of the way, give your underlings some rope, and hope they do not hang you in the process.

Once you have delegated and clearly explained their tasks, assignments, and responsibilities to your staff, let them perform. You will know soon enough whether or not they are up to the job. Keep your "kibitzing" instincts to yourself. Who knows, your employees might surprise you.

199. GET OUT OF THE WAY

Micromanaging is a great way to lose sight of the ultimate objective and organizational goals, as well as to lose the respect of your staff. It almost never works and lends itself to major frustration. Nobody is perfect. No business is perfect. The best we can all do is strive for perfection while acknowledging that this kind of striving will always be with us.

Your attorneys need freedom to innovate, to experiment with new ways of doing things. You will never know what they might produce for you and your organization if you don't permit them enough wiggle room to try. 3M, one of the great companies in this country, actively encourages its employees to be creative and even sets aside time to permit their creative juices to flow. If an employee comes up with something intriguing, there is even an opportunity for that person to profit from the company's marketing success.

Remember my story about the young attorney who snagged the Russian government as a client for his firm? He would never have been able to do this without some flexibility on his firm's part.

In contrast, one of my clients was an associate with a large law firm, a stodgy place where partners were gods and associates were charged with grinding out billable hours, and where everyone knew his place. My client, however, was a very impatient, creative sort of person, and one day he took it upon himself to snare a large client for his firm, hoping that his innovative marketing effort would win him points along the way. He was successful and brought in all of the environmental law business generated by a Fortune 50 corporation! An enormous coup for a partner anywhere, much less a lowly associate.

When he announced the new client to his practice group manager, was the latter pleased? Quite the contrary. He was (1) appalled that a mere associate had the chutzpah to go out and make this kind of "rain," something that, traditionally, only partners did, and (2) soon got around to battling with his partners over who among them would be credited with bringing in this huge client. There was no question that my client, the lowly associate, would not get any credit at all. In fact, the audacity he displayed put his job in jeopardy. Ultimately, he left and/or was thrown out of the firm. Soon thereafter, the firm closed its doors. The Fortune 50 client was so big that, had his manager handled this situation with intelligence, the firm might still be prospering today.

200. GET THE BEST EQUIPMENT YOU CAN LAY YOUR HANDS ON

State-of-the-art technology can make up for a lot: speed, flexibility, time efficiencies, you name it. In the modern business world, these are essential, and with new products popping up on the market every few months at plummeting prices, equipment buys become a nonissue. The payback time will be measured in weeks for most such upgrades.

Top-of-the-line equipment is required not only in the office, but also in the homes of your staff if you expect them to take work home. Use your lawyerly persuasive abilities to win this technology and any upgrades for your staff.

201. DON'T BE AFRAID TO CORRECT . . .

Everybody makes mistakes. If one of your employees messes up, call him or her into your office, point out what was done wrong, and suggest how to make it right. You will be doing both the employee and yourself a favor. Don't defer this important but often uncomfortable task. If you wait too long, bad habits become ingrained, memories become vague, and excuses have time to be honed.

Make sure you document your corrective discussion and put a copy of your memo in the employee's file. In these times of rampant employment litigation, it is important to have a record, should you have to bring—or defend—a more formal personnel action against the wayward employee.

202. . . . BUT DO SO PRIVATELY

If you must correct, critique, or criticize an employee, always do it privately, behind closed doors. It is a major distraction if you grump around the office muttering or shouting publicly about an employee's transgressions or assumed failings. It is also a guaranteed way to lose the respect of your entire staff.

203. DON'T JUST MANAGE . . . LEAD!

A good manager is not merely a manager or a cautious caretaker. He or she is, above all, a leader, someone whose qualities are such that other people will willingly follow him or her into the maelstrom.

While this entire chapter is really about leadership, I have distilled in this section the 25 essential attributes that I believe define a leader:

1. *Leaders are visionaries.* They have a set of goals that they intend to achieve. The bar is set high, but not unrealistically high.
2. *They think about the future and plan how to get there from here.* Even in a publicly traded company that must report its results every quarter, they strategize for the long term.
3. *They impart a sense of mission.* Leaders make sure that their staffs understand the organization's and department's missions and how they intend to achieve them.
4. *They are able to formulate a sense of direction.* Leaders are able to distill complex organizational aims into an understandable and cohesive picture.

5. *They are pragmatic.* Leaders are not hidebound by ideology. They are only interested in what works.

6. *They plan for both the best and the worst cases.* Leaders plan for both success and failure and always have a fallback plan for the latter.

7. *They study the past for keys to the future.* Leaders learn from what has gone before and factor past successes and failures into their thinking.

8. *They do more than just maintain.* Leaders always try to improve operations.

9. *They are brave.* They are willing to take risks after study has concluded that risks are warranted.

10. *They challenge convention.* Rather than copycatting the competition, a leader innovates and looks for new, faster, and more efficient ways to do things.

11. *They are careful.* Leaders do not rush headlong into something without thinking it through.

12. *They encourage dissent.* Leaders are comfortable enough in their own skin to be open to objections from their staff.

13. *They encourage ideas from their staff.* A leader knows that the marketplace of ideas is immensely valuable. He or she also understands that intellectual ferment is the brew of success.

14. *They give credit where credit is due.* If someone deserves a pat on the back, it is given freely, with enthusiasm, and publicly.

15. *They are respectful.* Leaders do not verbally abuse anyone.

16. *They motivate.* Leaders create excitement about projects and future growth of both individuals and the organization.

17. *They lead by example.* Leaders show the way. This is the best motivator.

18. *They are willing to get "down and dirty" and lend a hand when a hand is needed.* They are not reluctant to jump into any job within their responsibility parameter if the occasion requires.
19. *They are decisive.* A well-thought-out decision, once taken, moves forward to implementation without hesitation.
20. *They praise when praise is warranted.* Leaders do not withhold praise. They dole it out when appropriate.
21. *They punish when necessary.* Leaders do not let bad behavior or poor performance slide.
22. *They are fair.* Leaders do not play favorites. They treat everyone equally and as mature individuals.
23. *They have personal integrity.* A leader's sense of right and wrong is unambiguous. They live their values.
24. *They have an open door.* Leaders encourage their employees to come to them with their suggestions and their concerns.
25. *They nurture and build.* Leaders encourage good behavior, increased knowledge, and superior performance, and ask for more.

I elaborate on some of the most important leadership attributes below.

204. BE A RISK MANAGER

Risk management is one of those hot buzzwords of today's workplace. In addition to its popularity, it is also a good idea. Risk managers, basically, go around *identifying potential problems* and *taking steps to alleviate them* before they blow up in someone's face.

In your managerial capacity, you should apply the principles of risk management on four levels:

1. Looking out for Number One (yourself)
2. Looking out for your practice group/department
3. Looking out for your boss
4. Looking out for your organization

205. FIND AND KEEP GOOD PEOPLE

Finding good attorneys and support employees is difficult in any economy, even a dismal one where the market is flooded with individual attorneys with impressive résumés. Unfortunately, you cannot survive or succeed as a manager without them. That means that you have to invest the time and effort necessary to assemble the best possible staff.

While academic performance is an important factor, it is not necessarily the only factor. Two attorneys who worked for me at the same time demonstrated this very clearly. One was an honor graduate of a top law school. The other was a middle-of-the-class graduate of a law school far down in the national rankings. I hired both at roughly the same time and gave them similar assignments. The first attorney thought that he could get by on his academic credentials and acted a bit arrogant toward the rest of my staff. His colleague realized early on that he would have to study and work very hard in order to succeed. He did and he succeeded admirably while also becoming well liked by the staff. Attorney Number One never "got it."

Once you find that rarity, a really good employee, do whatever it takes to retain him or her. It will be worth it.

Take time up front to put together the best staff you can. Also the most compatible one. Investing time and effort in initial hiring decisions will pay big dividends later on, mainly in terms of the trouble you will avoid, not to mention not having to go through the unpleasantness of the hiring process more often than you would like.

Intelligent recruiting and hiring takes some effort: you need to accurately identify your needs, prepare the proper job advertisement, screen prospective applicants, interview them in-depth, carefully check their backgrounds and references, deter-mine if you like them as people, and assess their compatibility with your existing staff and organization.

206. COMMUNICATE UP AND DOWN

One of the biggest complaints I hear from disgruntled attorneys who come to me for career transition counseling is that no one ever tells them what is really going on in their organization: "I never get to see the whole picture."

Your employees will appreciate being in the know. It will give them a lift and make them feel more a part of the overall mission of the organization. They will work harder and better to achieve the organization's goals.

Similarly, your own supervisors have to know what you are doing, not only for their comfort, but for yours. If you work for an organization that does not have formal reporting, institute your own. Ask to meet with your supervisor once a week to review work. Provide a "weekly activities report."

207. MOTIVATE

Supervisors have to be a lot like athletic coaches. Occasionally, they are called upon to give a halftime pep talk. You don't have to be Knute Rockne, exhorting his Notre Dame players to win one for the Gipper, in order to be a good motivator. Similarly, you don't have to invoke the Golden Dome, the long tradition of Notre Dame or the Yankees or Papa Bear and the Monsters of the Midway, or bite the head off a live chicken, in order to pump up your staff or get the point across. Sometimes the quiet ones do it best. Tony Dungy, the recently retired coach of the NFL's Indianapolis Colts, is the epitome of someone who was able to motivate his players without going postal. The Colts, not surprisingly, won more games than any other team during his tenure.

Much of what constitutes successful motivation is clarifying missions and goals and demonstrating to your staff that you care about them and feel that the work they are doing has both value and a larger purpose.

208. FACILITATE

Make it easy for your staff to perform well. Look for bottlenecks to them getting their jobs done and remove them. If your new marketing director needs business cards in order to do her job, don't obstruct, don't delay. Get her the cards and have done with it.

If the technology your people are compelled to use is three generations behind the times, and their efficiency and productivity show it, lobby with higher management for new and faster machines. Demonstrate to your bosses how this small expense will increase the bottom line.

209. TREAT YOUR STAFF FAIRLY

The supervisor-employee relationship is a complex one, replete with all sorts of opportunities for abuse—much of it inadvertent—on both sides. The natural inclination is for supervisors to favor certain employees over others. It is an inclination to be avoided at all costs.

There are other, mainstream ways to reward good employees without overtly favoring them at the expense of—and to the detriment of your relationship with—others. Raises, better benefits (within the ridiculous restrictions of the law), promotions, bonuses, etc. Good employees who perform well and have a positive attitude should be rewarded.

The problem becomes aggravated when the favored employee is not necessarily the superperformer. At least there is, arguably, justification for favoring the superstar who is also the supervisor's fair-haired boy or girl. Even that tenuous justification goes down the toilet when the favorite is a lousy performer. That kind of situation can disrupt the workplace in a major way and ultimately cost you, the supervisor, your job.

210. STAND UP FOR YOUR TEAM

If you do not advocate on behalf of your staff, no one else will. And that means that they—and you—will lose out to your internal competition, always getting the short end of the stick.

Moreover, you will lose the respect of your team, and that will make your leadership job all that much tougher. Their respect is often the only thing that keeps things humming, after all.

When I was in the army, I briefly had a squad leader who was afraid of his own shadow. When one of the platoon officers tried to stick it to our squad, our squad leader invariably knuckled under, often even volunteering us for the most distasteful assignments. We would be slogging around in garbage while the other squads were out partying or relaxing.

Needless to say, it did not take long for us to lose all respect for our so-called leader. And we quickly discovered that we could be disrespectful to his face with impunity. There were no consequences at all. Our contempt knew no bounds, and as a result, he got to the point where he was completely unable to get us to do anything. We underperformed for him on purpose, not caring a whit whether he looked bad in the eyes of his superiors or not.

What the poor fellow discovered, after all of his sucking up to his superiors to our detriment, was that his misguided approach badly hurt his career. Others got promoted while he did not. Others got choice assignments while he got the dregs. Had this been 20 years later, he would surely have been drummed out of the army altogether.

211. BE CONSISTENT

One of the most disrupting things that can happen in the workplace is constant uncertainty about the boss's intentions. In no time at all, everyone becomes sufficiently distracted so that no work of any consequence ever gets done. This is a classic phenomenon in government, where many managers come into the job with no supervisory experience or training whatsoever, and the problem is compounded by the monumental problems associated with getting rid of civil service incompetents.

You can avoid a lot of problems if you demonstrate reliability, keep surprises to a minimum, and give your troops a sense of direction and purpose.

212. DON'T FRATERNIZE

The armed services think fraternization among officers and enlisted men and women is a criminal offense. And they are right. If you become too chummy with the troops you may later have to ask to risk their lives, you will have a supremely agonizing time asking them to take that kind of risk, and they may not take you seriously because you have become their "buddy." Consequently, fraternization, even under the most innocuous circumstances, is inherently frowned upon in the military.

While the black-and-white nature of the military environment in general, and combat in particular, does not exist in most workplaces, the precept against fraternization still makes some sense. You may not have to ask them to dodge bullets and mortars for their country or their fellow soldiers, but you may have to ask them to do some unpleasant or discomfiting things. It is a lot easier to make this kind of request or to order something like this if you are not bosom buddies. It is also a lot less distracting and offensive to your employees to have to do things they may not like if you have not broken bread together or shared a beer after hours.

I realize that this advice is directly contrary to the prevailing opinions and edicts of today's "flat organization" and "empowerment" management consultants. The only argument I have on my side is 10,000 years of the history of organizations and organizational effectiveness. So judge accordingly.

213. PRAISE WHEN WARRANTED

Everyone needs the psychic pleasure afforded by the occasional word of praise. It makes every party to the praised transaction feel good. There are studies that show that praise is as much a motivator of high performance as money.

Be the kind of manager who gives credit when credit is due and accords his or her employees a verbal pat on the head once in a while. You will be surprised at the tangible attitudinal and performance results.

214. REWARD THE WINNERS

If one of your employees does something truly outstanding, exceptional, or meritorious, make sure he or she is rewarded for it. If that means you have to go to bat for your superb staff member, do it. The fact that you did will be remembered by the rest of your staff, regardless of your success in wresting a suitable acknowledgment out of higher management, and you will be all the more respected for it.

Early in my legal career, I recommended a major alteration in the way my office conducted a central part of its business. My recommendation was accepted and implemented, resulting in a savings of several hundred thousand dollars per year. My boss put me in for a monetary reward through the office's formal "Suggestion Awards Program."

Two things happened as a result of his efforts: First, he won my undying loyalty and respect, especially since, when crunch time came, he fought very hard to get me what he felt was my just reward. Second, when I did not get it (it went instead to my boss's own supervisor who had resisted my suggestion from the beginning, then took credit for it when the anticipated savings were realized), I resolved never again to work for an organization that did not appreciate me. Rather, I would work for myself, where I would rise and fall completely on my own merits, without having to worry about what other folks did.

215. DON'T LET PROBLEMS FESTER

Nip problems in the bud. Whatever the issue, the longer you let it go, the worse it will surely become, until it develops into such a big distraction that your people are not getting any work done at all, and organizational progress grinds to a screeching halt.

There is another facet to acting quickly when it comes to putting out fires: employees have great radar where their colleagues are concerned. If they think someone is getting away with something, you are the one who will lose respect if you do nothing about it. And your employees' respect is an immensely valuable commodity, one that you can take to the bank, literally and figuratively. No one enjoys seeing a coworker putting one over on the boss and getting away with it. You will earn a lot of points with your staff if you put out fires as soon as you see smoke.

If one of your staff is a chronic late arriver at work, for example, make sure you put a stop to that behavior as soon as you see a pattern. Employees get very easily distracted if they think someone is pulling a fast one on you and you are not doing anything about it.

216. THINK GREEN

While I have always been wary of fads (total quality management, zero-base budgeting, flat management, team-building), and glib labeling (empowerment, infrastructure, stakeholders), climate change and its ominous implications are different. Global warming is not a management consulting fad. It is likely here to stay for a good long while and is already being incorporated into public and private sector decision making. Globally and domestically, there is a broad public consensus that this is an important issue that needs attention.

Consequently, it can only boost your career to "think green." There are simple and creative ways to do this and to cement your reputation as a manager who recommends and initiates in this cutting-edge area. For example, the closer you can get to a paper-less office, the greener—and less costly—your operation will be. Each year the average American throws out almost 2,500 pounds of paper at home. The amount of paper that office workers discard probably dwarfs that amount. Discarded paper usually winds up in a landfill, and landfills are filling up rapidly. Moreover, paper usage denudes the planet of trees, which are the best defense against global warming because each tree takes an enormous amount of carbon dioxide out of the atmosphere.

Another easy initiative is to analyze your office lighting system for green opportunities. Replacing lightbulbs with energy-efficient ones, instituting policies that encourage employees to turn off lights when they leave their workspaces, etc. are easy green fixes.

These suggestions just scratch the surface. Remember, little things like this stick in the organizational memory.

217. TAKE A STEP BACK

Europeans have the right idea. They know when and how to relax. Americans have lost that ability, if they ever had it in the first place.

Periodically, you should stop, take a few deep breaths, and just get away from it all for a while. Do something totally unrelated to work. I don't care who you are, you are not superhuman. All of us have to recharge our batteries from time to time.

This is even more important for leaders than for your employees. If you are any kind of leader-manager at all, you naturally take work home with you or at least worry about it away from the office. You probably even lose sleep over your work. No one can do that constantly, without let-up, and still be effective. After a long stint of being "on" all the time, you are bound to lose something.

When you feel this happening, it is a good time to take some time off and distract yourself. You will be surprised to find how much clearer your thinking is when you come back, reenergized, from your break.

Chapter 7

Dispensable...
In Spite of Yourself

*Y*OU HAVE DONE EVERYTHING *right, strictly followed all of the advice in this book, and rendered yourself as indispensable to your employer as any employee could possibly be . . . and it is not enough. You are still in jeopardy of losing your job, but through no fault of your own. This kind of misfortune can—and does—happen. Despite all of your heroics at work, you are still in trouble.*

This chapter discusses the circumstances beyond your control that you have to watch out for and that can render you dispensable, and what you can do to mitigate the pain and ease the transition. You will discover that, despite the hammer blow of a layoff, the steps you have taken toward indispensability will carry over and give you a powerful advantage in the competitive legal job market.

218. NEVER ASSUME THAT YOUR JOB IS 100 PERCENT SECURE

Fifty percent of the companies on the Fortune 500 list were not there 30 years ago. Giant companies such as Wal-Mart, The Limited, Waste Management Inc., Blockbuster, Apple, Federal Express, Toys "R" Us, and AOL were either tiny or did not even exist back then. In fact, 45 companies—almost 10 percent of the entire list—were dropped from the list in 2008. In all likelihood, that number will increase in 2009. As this is written, General Motors does not even make the Fortune 1,000 list.

Thirty years ago, 17 of the 20 largest banks in the world were U.S. institutions. Today, only three U.S. banks make the list.

In 1975, the 10 best-selling cars in the United States were all manufactured by domestic automakers. Today, 4 are Japanese.

Twenty-five years ago, the Big Three television networks (ABC, CBS, and NBC) controlled almost a 100 percent share of the U.S. viewing audience. Today, they are down to 32 percent.

All of this means that we live in a world of constant—and accelerating—change. Look at any industry and what you see is tremendous flux. As we learned on September 11, 2001, and then once again in the Great Recession of 2008 and beyond, change and upheaval are the only constants, and uncertainty is just around the corner. A person who ignores these realities does so at his or her peril.

Who would have thought as recently as early 2008 that the bedrock financial and manufacturing industries that built this country and fueled our economy would be on the ropes, in danger of disappearing altogether only a year later? The lesson is, you may be indispensable, but your company and your industry are not.

219. CONTINUALLY UPDATE YOUR RÉSUMÉ ... ON PAPER ...

The very worst time to put together a résumé is when you have no choice. The best time to put together a résumé is *before* it becomes necessary. You can best describe your job accomplishments when they are fresh in your mind, you are feeling pretty good about yourself, and you are unfettered by negative thoughts. Your accomplishments and results are what will sell you to your new employer.

Take time periodically to review your résumé and bring it up-to-date. Keep a file marked "résumé additions" in which you store records of all of the good things that you have achieved at work.

220. ... AND ONLINE

There are numerous résumé databases on the Internet. In addition to exclusively legal résumé databases, there are a large number of specialized legal and law-related job databases that permit members of certain organizations to post their résumés, such as the following:

- Association for Conflict Resolution (*www.acrnet.org*)
- Higher Education Jobs (*www.higheredjobs.com*)
- Association of Corporate Counsel (*www.acc.com*)
- Compliance Jobs (*www.jobsinthemoney.com*)
- U.S. Government (*www.usajobs.gov*)
- Contract and Procurement (*www.ncmajobs.com*)
- Energy Industry Jobs (*www.energyjobsnetwork.com*)
- Immigration Law (*http://careers.aila.org/hr*)
- Intellectual Property (*www.aipla.org*)
- Licensing and Technology Transfer (*www.autm.net*)

Most of these will allow you to post your résumé free of charge. Some will even permit you to post more than one résumé, which is ideal for anyone who wants to have résumés with different emphases to target different industries and employment sectors.

A very important point: *Choose online résumé databases that promise to keep your résumé confidential—that means that you are not identified to the employer until you decide that the time has come to reveal yourself.*

Once a résumé is entered in one of these databases, employers can search the databases either free of charge or for a fee. A large number of employers are doing this, and if you play this card right, you could be extracted from the database and given serious scrutiny by a prospective employer.

How do you play this card right? *By making certain that you enter the keywords in your online résumé that will get your document extracted by an interested employer.* This means putting yourself in the shoes of an employer and analyzing which keywords would be likely to be entered by an employer seeking someone with your background and skills.

One of my legal career transition counseling clients was an attorney who worked in the competition policy office of a large government agency. He entered his résumé in an online database and, despite his excellent qualifications, he never received any expression of interest from an employer. When he presented me with the résumé that he had posted online, I noticed that the word "antitrust" was nowhere to be found in the document, despite the fact that he was a very accomplished antitrust lawyer and his work was heavily antitrust oriented. He had failed to anticipate that private law firms and corporate legal offices think in terms of "antitrust," not "competition." Within days of revising his online résumé to include the term "antitrust," he received inquiries from several law firms.

221. BUILD AND NURTURE YOUR NETWORK

Everyone claims that most jobs are filled by networking. While a decidedly unproven assertion, networking is, nevertheless, very important to any job search. Professional contacts and strategically located friends and acquaintances can open doors that might otherwise be closed to you and can serve as information sources that are invaluable. I know of many instances where networking contacts were able to provide advance information about job opportunities long before they became public information.

Unfortunately, most job applicants—legal job applicants in particular, for reasons I have never understood—find networking distasteful, stressful, and discomfiting, which makes their job hunting that much more difficult. Worse, they wait until they absolutely have to find a new job to begin building a network. Just like with the need to prepare a résumé in haste, this is the worst possible time to begin building and nurturing a network.

It is essential to begin building and to continue cultivating your network *before* you need it. Aside from being prepared before the roof falls in, a preexisting network is a lot easier to develop when you *don't* need it.

There are a variety of ways to do this, such as staying in touch with professional colleagues with whom you come into contact, communicating periodically with classmates and teachers, joining and actively participating in professional societies, going to conferences and meetings, joining alumni associations, writing articles for publication that require you to interview experts, etc.

Here is a list of the people whom you should consider for your network:

- Friends
- Relatives

- Friends of friends
- Friends of relatives
- Neighbors
- Friends of neighbors
- Fellow academic alumni
- Teachers and school administrators
  - Law school
  - Graduate school
  - College
  - Other
- Current classmates
- Current employer (if she or he knows about your job search)
- Colleagues at work
  - Current job
  - Prior jobs
- Workplace alumni
  - Current job
  - Prior jobs
- Former employers
- Other professional colleagues
- Opposing counsel
- Judges and hearing officers
- Current and former clients
- Job interviewers (whom you impressed)
- Political contacts (if any)
- Members of clubs and organizations to which you belong (such as bar associations, community and cultural groups, church/synagogue/mosque/ashram, etc., PTAs, athletic teams, and other volunteer or community groups)

An increasing number of attorneys are turning to online social networking as an alternative to the hard and often uncomfortable work involved in one-to-one networking. They are using Facebook (*www.facebook.com*), LinkedIn (*www.linkedin.com*), Lawyrs.net (*www.lawyrs.net*), and by-invitation-only LegalOnRamp (*www.legalonramp.com*), among other websites, where they post comments about themselves, set up profiles, join groups, make contacts, etc. To date, this appears to be a poor substitute for one-to-one marketing. Moreover, it has the potential to be dangerous. Employers increasingly check these sites to see what they can discover about prospective legal job candidates. Sometimes what they see on the site is reason enough not to make a job offer.

Worse, current employers are also becoming more attuned to the existence of social networking sites and are going there to see what their current employees are posting. If they find your résumé there, they will likely not be happy.

Of course, you will want to be careful whom you contact, given that your job search might be clandestine (i.e., without the knowledge of your current employer) and will, to a great extent, depend on your relationships with some of the possible contacts on this list.

Once you have built a suitable network, make sure you maintain contact with its members and that they are kept aware of your professional development and achievements.

222. HEAD THEM OFF AT THE PASS

If you are able to anticipate that your demise may be imminent, consider proposing an *outsourcing* arrangement to your employer. Outsourcing means moving from being an employee to becoming an independent contractor. Technically, you would be performing the same job, but your employment relationship would be altered.

Several years ago, the U.S. government was about to deep-six a large group of several hundred employees who performed background investigations of prospective federal employees. Instead, the affected employees proposed to the government that they form a company and provide the services from outside, and at favorable rates to the government. This proved to be quite successful, especially since the new private company was able to promote its services to private sector government contractors who also needed them in order to vet new hires who required security clearances. The private contractors got a firm that knew the government investigation and clearance process backward and forward. The government saved a lot of money, and the new firm's employees retained their jobs. A win-win situation for all concerned.

The economics of outsourcing work are rather favorable to employers. If the employer does not have to pay benefits, he or she may well be interested in your proposal. Certainly, you would be earning less compensation than you do as a full-time employee, but consider the alternative. Moreover, outsourcing is a means of securing financing (the ongoing paycheck) for your entrepreneurial spirit. You may be able to perform some or all of the same functions for another employer interested in saving money via outsourcing.

Try to recognize outsourcing opportunities before they mature. A strong indicator of outsourcing potential is if the work is periodic and the staff handling the function is not consistently busy. Another is if your analysis clearly shows that you can save your employer money.

You may, of course, propose other compensation—or flexible work arrangements—to your employer: hourly, fixed-fee, project-based, percentage of savings to the employer, telecommuting, half-time or part-time, etc.

If you think the ax might soon fall, this is the best time to wax creative.

223. IT ISN'T OVER UNTIL IT'S OVER ...
AND OVER ... AND OVER

Looking back, I consider what I am about to tell you one of my greatest accomplishments as a legal career transition counselor:

A very large national law firm sent me a candidate who was being terminated despite her stellar background and achievements as a securities litigator. She specialized in several rather exotic practice subspecialties, and her firm had determined that they did not want to build out this particular practice.

She was not only highly intelligent, but also extremely personable and friendly and very presentable. In short, she had it all.

She did not at all fit the "template" of terminated attorneys from this particular firm, based on the attorneys they had previously sent to me. I was befuddled by the firm's wanting to let her go after investing seven years in her career and could not determine what the hidden problem could be.

My standard opening in almost every case where a candidate is being laid off is to pose the following questions: "Is there anything that you could do to remain with the firm?" "Are there any firm practice areas to which you could transfer your skills and experience?" Sometimes, when I have felt that the firm might be making a mistake and when the candidate authorized me, I took it upon myself to advocate for retention on behalf of a candidate (usually to no avail).

As we proceeded down the counseling road, she often complained that her workload at the firm was such that she could not find time to engage in a job search. In fact, as our professional relationship progressed, her workload grew more intense.

The time came when she found herself in her last week at the firm without having made much progress toward a job change. When she came to see me on Friday—her last day at the firm—her first comment was that she was in the middle of preparing for a very major litigation and that no one at the firm had bothered to assume responsibility for the case or client.

That was when I came up with a novel idea: I suggested to her that she report to work on the following Monday morning as if nothing had happened and continue to forge ahead on her trial preparation. She was taken aback, to say the least, but I convinced her that she had nothing to lose by trying my suggested approach. She said she would think about it over the weekend.

On Monday around the end of the business day, she called me to report that she had, in fact, gone to work that morning and spent most of the day developing her case, when her practice group leader walked into her office and assigned her a new project!

Today, she is a partner in that same firm. No one had ever mentioned her "termination" in the intervening time period.

224. DON'T SHRINK WITH YOUR INDUSTRY

If you work in a declining economic sector, the time to think about doing something else was yesterday. Being a telephone operator during the telecommunications revolution is like going to Henry Ford for a job if you are a career blacksmith. It's not going to happen.

Industries undergoing heavy automation, such as banking, shipping, printing, and publishing, will soon need only bare-bones staff. A giant oil tanker too big to go through the Suez Canal is so sophisticated a technological wonder that it can now be manned by only six people! Get started early in preparing to "re-career" yourself.

225. LOOK BEFORE YOU LEAP

Even given everything that's been said here about moving on from an ailing company, think at least twice before you sever your employment relationship. Even if you believe that a downsizing—or worse—is imminent, it may be much better if you stick it out.

It is more difficult to get a new job if you are unemployed than if you are currently working. Unemployment leaves a "mark of Cain" on your forehead, and while that mark is fainter today than it was 10 years ago, it is still there. Besides, you never know what might happen to save the situation at the 11th hour. Frequently, for example, a "white knight" comes along at the last minute to save a takeover candidate company from being absorbed.

226. DON'T BURN BRIDGES

A very large international corporation that hired us to handle some of its outplacement work discharged several of its Texas attorneys during a downsizing. Two individuals with the same job responsibilities handled the terminations in very different—and sharply contrasting—ways. One was very public about her bitterness and outrage and pulled no punches when discussing her superiors with outsiders. The other maintained excellent relations with his colleagues and asked his superiors in the company for any career and job-hunting advice they might have for him. In addition, he offered to assist them with any short-term projects that necessitated his expertise during his transition to a new job.

Such a consulting opportunity did in fact arise and he was asked if he would mind commuting weekly to California for two months to handle some company work on-site. He did so, and at the end of his short-term contract, was offered a full-time job with another division of the company with which he had come into contact during the consultancy.

The bitter employee, in contrast, left the company on her termination date, having so alienated her bosses that she was denied extended outplacement services when every other terminated employee was granted them.

If you need to vent about your job loss, do it outside of the workplace and in a context where your comments will be protected and not become public.

This is not easy. Basically, you need to exercise supreme self-control under the most extreme duress. You are being advised to be nice and friendly to the misguided, mean-spirited know-nothings who just fired you!

That's exactly right. In this market and these economic times, the old so-called mafia adage—"it's nothing personal"—before someone is "eliminated," applies equally to the job market. And more often than not, it's true. It isn't personal. It's a fact of business life.

This bit of advice could also be called "what goes around comes around." You never know when you might run into these guys again. They might even be able to do you a great deal of good if you stay polite and civil and courteous. We have often had counseling clients whose firms have actually gone the extra mile to gain them entry to hard-to-see executives of other firms where they have ultimately wound up.

If you raise a big stink, go ballistic, or mope around like a gloomy Gus, these same people can do you a lot of harm. Besides, feeling persecuted and grumping about it won't get you one millimeter farther ahead. It is guaranteed to make you feel even worse.

227. STUDY ENTREPRENEURIALISM

With sudden and unanticipated job loss affecting millions of people, literally everyone has to be prepared to go it alone, should that become necessary. As a college football star (who is studying business with a view to becoming an entrepreneur once his playing days are over) recently put it: "When you own something, it's harder for people to take it away from you."

There are a slew of excellent books about starting and managing your own solo practice. In addition, the U.S. Small Business Administration can provide you with a wealth of good information about what being a businessperson requires. You may also wish to subscribe to the growing number of good specialty magazines on the subject, such as *Entrepreneur* and *Inc.*

Regardless of how you go about studying the topic, the point is to be prepared in the event you decide, or the decision is made for you, to take the plunge.

228. CONSIDER INVESTING IN YOURSELF

If you took the advice in the previous section and feel up to speed on what it takes to become an entrepreneur, now may be the time to seriously consider an investment in your future. There are a lot of opportunities to become a sole practitioner or legal entrepreneur today that did not exist as recently as a decade ago. Technology and plummeting costs have made these options available to almost everyone, and at very low costs of entry.

Many of my clients became sole practitioners because they were downsized out of their legal jobs. They went into a wide variety of legal arenas, including general practice, litigation, litigation support (brief writing, preparing pleadings, etc., for other practitioners with spillover work), sports agenting, litigation management consulting, mediation, and many more.

One of my attorney clients started his own Internet business advising benefits claimants on how to go about preparing and presenting their claims. His practice began with Social Security Disability Income claims and expanded into workers' compensation claims and general insurance claims. He was able to do this under the Rules of Professional Conduct because this kind of claims representation does not require someone to be an attorney, despite the fact that these proceedings and determinations are very much legal ones.

One very good place that attorneys can turn for valuable consulting advice on starting and managing a law practice is the law practice management section of a state bar. Virtually every state bar association maintains this resource. The kind of consulting advice that you can receive from such a section is often worth tens of thousands of dollars.

Local colleges and universities often sponsor small business centers where entrepreneurs can go for advice and assistance with such things as crafting business plans to present to prospective investors. The small business centers serve as laboratories where students can gain experience with business problems in the real world, i.e., your world.

Going into business for yourself is still one of the linchpins of the American dream. If you are prepared and committed to succeeding, job-loss time may be just the time to do it.

229. ASK FOR SEVERANCE

A number of companies have established severance payment formulas that kick in during a downsizing. Severance payment obligations may be part of a management-union collective bargaining agreement, an employment contract, or if not documented, part of company policy. If one of these three scenarios is the case, then you do not have to do any demanding, requesting, or negotiating in order to receive severance payments.

While there is no uniform approach to severance, the amount and the number of payments are generally tied to the duration of your employment. One simple formula that applies is one month's severance for every year of employment. Under that scheme, a 12-year employee would get a full year of severance (equal to 100 percent of salary). Severance generally means that an employee who earns $5,000 per month would receive a monthly check for the same $5,000 (minus, of course, federal and state withholding, Social Security contribution, Medicare contribution, etc.).

The importance of severance cannot be overstated. Severance payments almost always dwarf what is available through unemployment insurance.

If your organization does not have a documented or undocumented severance policy, the time to ask for severance is when you receive notice of termination. While it may seem odd to make such a statement, the power equation at the time of such notice is not as obvious as you might believe. Obviously, being told that you are being let go makes you feel about as vulnerable and weak vis-à-vis your employer as it is possible to be. However, your employer is also at his or her most vulnerable at this time. How can that be?

Employers are universally terrified of two kinds of lawsuits: wrongful termination suits and antidiscrimination suits. Tens of thousands of each are filed with the courts every year by employees who feel that they have been unjustifiably released. Employers might be very eager to do whatever is necessary to insulate themselves against such potentially damaging litigation. A savvy employer will also take the opportunity to have you sign a severance agreement in which you commit to refrain from suing for your dismissal.

230. REQUEST OUTPLACEMENT ASSISTANCE

More and more companies offer their terminated employees outplacement assistance. Don't confuse *outplacement* with *placement.* The former means help with job hunting and career transition when you lose your existing job. The latter means working through an executive search firm (a headhunter) to find a new job where the employer pays the headhunter for snaring you.

Outplacement is offered less for reasons of sympathy and compassion for the soon-to-be unemployed and more because employers are terrified of the very same lawsuits cited above. Outplacement is often intended to head off such suits.

Outplacement services can be a big help in finding a new job. A competent outplacement consultant can help you develop compelling résumés and cover letters, point you in the right direction, train you in effective interviewing, assist you in building a strong network of contacts, provide you with solid job information, and counsel you on negotiating a new employment agreement, which may include higher compensation.

If outplacement is offered, take full advantage of it. If it is not, request it when you receive notice of termination.

Some Final Words

S AY THAT YOU HAVE applied all of the recommendations in this book and survived a downsizing. Congratulations. Now you can relax, right?

Wrong!

As I said in the Introduction, you can *never* relax. Not in today's job environment. You always need to be "on" at work. Being indispensable needs to be a way of life.

The two common themes that run through these 230 principles that you can adopt and apply to make yourself indispensable—(1) common sense and (2) preparation—are not automatic. While simple, most people have a lot of difficulty applying these principles to their work situations. It takes the application of another fundamental principle: perspiration. Like learning how to ride a bicycle or drive a car, you need to internalize the basic principles of achieving excellence in the workplace so that they become second nature, things that you do not have to think about in order to execute. If you are able to do that, you will have created a platform—a takeoff point—that enables you to add the extra something that sets you completely apart, renders you indispensable, and to the extent possible, locks in job security, success, survival, and satisfaction.

Index

About the Author

RICHARD HERMANN, ESQ., received his JD from Cornell Law School, his BA from Yale, and is a Concord Law School professor specializing in legal career management.

He developed Concord's Legal Career Management course, a unique program for Concord's nontraditional working student population that provides guidance and resources as they look to blend their previous experience with their law degree. He was previously the founder and president of Federal Reports Inc., the leading provider of legal career information in the U.S., and co-founded AttorneyJobs.com.

He is also the author of *The Lawyer's Guide to Finding Success in Any Job Market.*